DISNEY · PIXAR
COMICS TREASURY

WALL·E

 **JOE BOOKS INC**

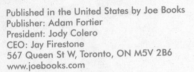 HarperCollins*Publishers*Ltd

Published in the United States by Joe Books
Publisher: Adam Fortier
President: Jody Colero
CEO: Jay Firestone
567 Queen St W, Toronto, ON M5V 2B6
www.joebooks.com

HarperCollins Books may be purchased for educational, business, or sales promotional use through our Special
Markets Department.

HarperCollins Publishers Ltd
2 Bloor Street East, 20th Floor
Toronto, Ontario, Canada
M4W 1A8

www.harpercollins.ca

Library and Archives Canada Cataloguing in Publication information is available upon request.

ISBN 978-1-443444-85-9 (HarperCollins Publishers Ltd edition, Canada)
ISBN 978-1-926516-01-1 (Joe Books edition, US)
First Joe Books and HarperCollins Publishers Ltd Editions: January 2015
3 5 7 9 10 8 6 4 2

Published in the United States by Joe Books, Inc.
Published in Canada by HarperCollins Publishers Ltd, by arrangement with Joe Books, Inc.

Printed in USA through Avenue4 Communications at Cenveo/Richmond, Virginia

For information regarding the CPSIA on this printed material, call: (203) 595-3636 and provide reference
#RICH - 602287.

Disney · PIXAR
COMICS TREASURY

BRAVE
ADAPTATION: ALESSANDRO FERRARI
LAYOUTS: EMILIO URBANO
PENCILS: MANUELA RAZZI
COLOR: GIUSEPPE FONTANA, MASSIMO ROCCA, ANGELA CAPOLUPO

CARS
ADAPTATION: ALESSANDRO SISTI
PENCILS: ANTONELLO DALENA
INKS: CRISTINA GIORGILLI
COLOR: MAURIZIO DE BELLIS, GIORGIO VALLORANI, DARIO CALABRIA
ART OPTIMIZATION & SUPPORT: DARIO CALABRIA, VALENTINO FORLINI, EMANUELE GRASSI, FABIO POCHET, FEDERICA SALFO
ADDITIONAL CONTRIBUTORS: STEFANO ATTARDI, CARLOTTA QUATTROCOLO, ANDREA CARLO RIPAMONTI, GIANMARCO VILLA

CARS 2
ADAPTATION: ALESSANDRO FERRARI
LAYOUT: ANTONELLO DALENA
PENCILS: VALENTINO FORLINI, EMILIO GRASSO, LUCA USAI
INKS: MICHELA FRARE
COLOR: PACO DESIATO
COLOR COORDINATION: TOMATOFARM
COVER ART: MARCO GHIGLIONE, STEFANO ATTARDI
ART SUPPORT: CRISTINA GIORGILLI, JASON PELTZ, TERESA QUEZADA GEER, MARINA IOVINE, ANGELO AMORELLI

FINDING NEMO
ADAPTATION: CHARLES BAZALDUA
LAYOUT / PENCILS / INKS: CLAUDIO SCIARRONE
COLOR: GABRIELLA MATTA, DAVIDE BALDONI
COVER ART: CLAUDIO SCIARRONE, GABRIELLA MATTA, DAVIDE BALDONI
ART OPTIMIZATION: DARIO CALABRIA

THE INCREDIBLES
ADAPTATION: GREGORY EHRBAR
LAYOUTS / PENCILS / INKS: GIOVANNI RIGANO
COLOR: GIORGIO VALLORANI
ART OPTIMIZATION: DARIO CALABRIA

MONSTERS UNIVERSITY
ADAPTATION: ALESSANDRO FERRARI
LAYOUTS / PENCILS: ELISABETTA MELARANCI
COLOR: LORENZO DE FELICI, ANNALISA LEONI, PACO DESIATO
ART COORDINATION: TOMATOFARM
COVER ART: ELISABETTA MELARANCI, LORENZO DE FELICI

MONSTERS, INC.

ADAPTATION: CHARLES BAZALDUA
LAYOUTS: CLAUDIO SCIARRONE
PENCILS: ELISABETTA MELARANCI AND ANNA MERLI
INKS: DAVIDE ZANNETTI AND SONIA MATRONE
COLOR: MARA DAMIANI AND ELENA M. NAGGI

RATATOUILLE

ADAPTATION: AUGUSTO MACCHETTO
LAYOUTS: EMILIO URBANO
CLEAN-UP: MARCO GENTILINI
INKS: MICHELA FRARE
COLOR: MAURIZIO DE BELLIS, HELGE VOGT, GIORGIO VALLORANI.
ART OPTIMIZATION: KAWAII STUDIO

TOY STORY

ADAPTATION: ALESSANDRO FERRARI
PENCILS / INKS: ETTORE GULA
COLOR: KAWAII CREATIVE STUDIO, LUCIO DE GIUSEPPE, MAURIZIO DE BELLIS
ART OPTIMIZATION: STEFANO ATTARDI
ADDITIONAL CONTRIBUTORS: ELISABETTA SEDDA

TOY STORY 2

ADAPTATION: ALESSANDRO FERRARI
PENCILS / INKS: ETTORE GULA
COLOR: KAWAII CREATIVE STUDIO
ART OPTIMIZATION: STEFANO ATTARDI
ADDITIONAL CONTRIBUTORS: ELISABETTA SEDDA

TOY STORY 3

ADAPTATION: ALESSANDRO FERRARI
PENCILS / INKS: ETTORE GULA
COLOR: KAWAII CREATIVE STUDIO
ART OPTIMIZATION: STEFANO ATTARDI, GIUSEPPE FONTANA
ADDITIONAL CONTRIBUTORS: PAOLA BERETTA, ELISABETTA SEDDA, LUCA USAI

UP

ADAPTATION: ALESSANDRO FERRARI
LAYOUT: EMILIO URBANO
CLEAN-UP: LUCA USAI
INKS: MICHELA FRARE, ROBERTA ZANOTTA
COLOR: LUCIO DE GIUSEPPE, GIUSEPPE FONTANA, KAWAII CREATIVE STUDIO, SILVANO SCOLARI, HELGE VOGT
ADDITIONAL CONTRIBUTORS: ALISA SCHMUHL, ELISABETTA SEDDA, FLAVIO CHIUMENTO

WALL-E

ADAPTATION: ALESSANDRO FERRARI
PENCILS / INKS: CLAUDIO SCIARRONE
COLOR: KAWAII CREATIVE STUDIO, MAURIZIO DE BELLIS
ART OPTIMIZATION: STEFANO ATTARDI, KAWAII CREATIVE STUDIO
ADDITIONAL CONTRIBUTORS: FEDERICA SALFO, LUCA USAI, GIOIA GABRIELLI, ELISABETTA SEDDA

WALL-E: RECHARGE

SCRIPT: J. TORRES
PENCILS / INKS: MORGAN LUTHI
COLORS: DIGIKORE STUDIOS
LETTERS: JOSE MACASOCOL, JR., DERON BENNETT

TABLE OF CONTENTS

JAIL

YOU SAVED THE DAY *AGAIN*, WOODY!

IT'S ANOTHER ADVENTURE-FILLED DAY FOR **ANDY DAVIS**...

...AND HIS **SPECIAL PAL.**

COME ON!

A DAY LOADED WITH SURPRISES...

WOW! COOL!

THIS LOOKS GREAT, MOM! CAN WE LEAVE THIS UP 'TIL WE MOVE?

WELL, SURE, **BIRTHDAY BOY!**

NOW, GO GET MOLLY. YOUR FRIENDS ARE GOING TO BE HERE ANY MINUTE.

IT'S PARTY TIME!

A MOMENT LATER, THE MEETING HAS JUST STARTED AND...

WHAT?!?

WADDA YA *MEAN*, THE PARTY'S *TODAY?!* HIS BIRTHDAY'S NOT 'TIL *NEXT WEEK!*

WHAT?!?

WELL, OBVIOUSLY HIS MOM WANTED TO HAVE THE PARTY BEFORE THE *MOVE.* I'M NOT WORRIED, *YOU* SHOULDN'T BE WORRIED.

BUT WHAT IF ANDY GETS ANOTHER DINOSAUR? A *MEAN* ONE?

HEY, LISTEN REX, *NO ONE'S* GETTING REPLACED.

I HATE TO BREAK UP THE STAFF MEETING BUT... *THEY'RE HERE!* BIRTHDAY GUESTS!

STAY CALM, EVERYONE! *HEY!*

WOAAA

MANY PRESENTS LATER...

OK, WE'RE ON THE LAST ONE *NOW*...

IT'S BIG...IT'S A... IT'S A *BOARD GAME!*

HALLELUJAH! YEAH!

DIDN'T I TELL YA? NOTHING TO WORR--

COME IN, MOTHER BIRD! MOM HAS PULLED A SURPRISE PRESENT FROM THE CLOSET!

ANDY'S OPENING IT. HE'S REALLY EXCITED ABOUT THIS ONE...

IT'S A HUGE PACKAGE. IT'S A...

CRRRCRRR

IT'S A *WHAT?* WHAT *IS* IT?

LET'S GO TO MY ROOM, *GUYS!*

!

RED ALERT! RED ALERT! ANDY IS COMING UPSTAIRS! RESUME YOUR POSITIONS, *NOW!*

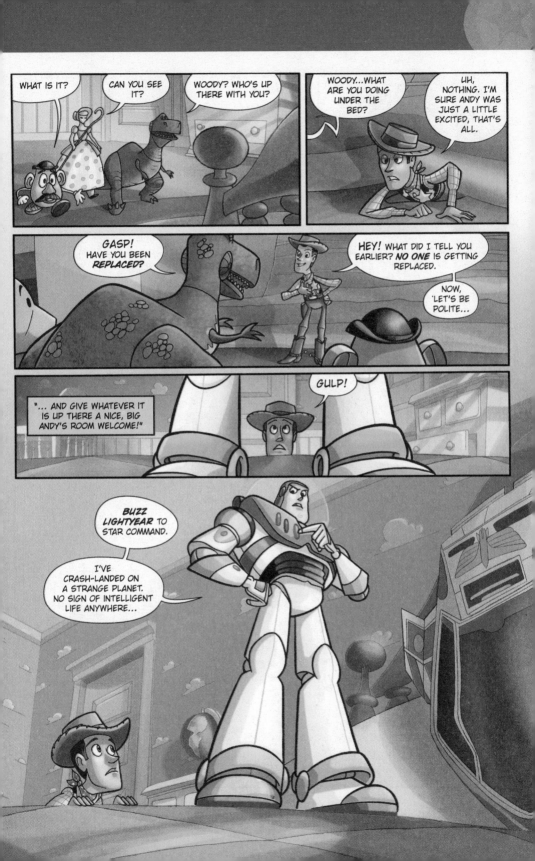

BUT OVER THE NEXT FEW DAYS...

...IT DOESN'T LOOK LIKE THINGS WILL EVER BE THE SAME AGAIN.

YOUR CHIEF, ANDY, INSCRIBED HIS NAME ON ME!

WITH PERMANENT INK, TOO!

ARF ARF ARF

...INCOMING!

?

21

OH, NO! *SID!*

I CAN'T BEAR TO WATCH ONE OF THESE AGAIN!

WHO IS IT *THIS* TIME?

A COMBAT CARL!

ARF

ARF

WHY IS THAT SOLDIER STRAPPED TO AN EXPLOSIVE DEVICE?

SID! HE *TORTURES* TOYS... JUST FOR FUN!

HE'S LIGHTING IT!

BOOM

THE SOONER WE MOVE, THE BETTER.

BUZZ!!!

THIS WAS NO ACCIDENT--BUZZ WAS *PUSHED*... BY *WOODY!*

NO! IT WAS AN ACCIDENT! C'MON, YOU...YOU GOTTA *BELIEVE* ME. I WAS...

OK, MOM, BE RIGHT DOWN. I'VE GOT TO GET BUZZ.

HEADS UP! ANDY'S COMING!

MOM, I CAN'T FIND HIM!

WELL, HONEY, JUST GRAB SOME OTHER TOY!

I COULDN'T FIND MY BUZZ. I KNOW I LEFT HIM RIGHT THERE.

HONEY, I'M SURE HE'S AROUND...

"...YOU'LL FIND HIM."

A LITTLE WHILE LATER...

CAN I HELP PUMP THE GAS, MOM?

SURE!

OH, GREAT. HOW AM I GONNA CONVINCE THOSE GUYS IT WAS AN ACCIDENT?

BUZZ! YOU'RE ALIVE!

GREAT! ANDY'LL TAKE US BACK AND THEN YOU CAN TELL EVERYONE THAT THIS WAS ALL JUST A BIG *MISTAKE!*

RIGHT, BUDDY?

I JUST WANT YOU TO KNOW THAT EVEN THOUGH YOU TRIED TO TERMINATE ME, REVENGE IS NOT AN IDEA WE PROMOTE ON MY PLANET.

OH, THAT'S GOOD!

BUT WE'RE NOT *ON* MY PLANET, *ARE* WE?

A FEW MINUTES LATER, HIDDEN ABOARD THE VAN...

SKREEE

...THE TWO TOYS REACH THEIR DESTINATION!

YOU ARE CLEARED TO ENTER. WELCOME TO *PIZZA PLANET.*

THE ENTRANCE IS HEAVILY GUARDED. WE NEED A WAY TO GET INSIDE...AND *THAT'S* A GREAT IDEA, WOODY!

?

TIC TIC TIC TIC TIC TIC

WHAT A *SPACE PORT!* NOW WE HAVE TO FIND A SHIP THAT'S HEADED FOR SECTOR 12...

OK, BUZZ, WHEN I SAY "GO," WE'RE GONNA JUMP IN THE BASKET...

ANDY!

BUT THE SPACE RANGER HAS FOUND THE **SPACE SHIP** HE WAS LOOKING FOR.

BUZZ! NO, **WAIT!**

CLIMBING ABOARD, HE ENCOUNTERS ITS STRANGE **PASSENGERS!**

A STRANGER!

FROM THE OUTSIDE!

GREETINGS! I'M BUZZ LIGHTYEAR! I NEED TO COMMANDEER YOUR VESSEL TO SECTOR 12. WHO'S IN CHARGE HERE?

THE CLAAAAAAW!

MEANWHILE, WOODY HAS REACHED THE SPACE CRANE TO GET BUZZ BACK, BUT SO HAS...

SID!

GET DOWN!

GOTCHA!

A BUZZ LIGHTYEAR! NO WAY!

VZZZ

BUZZ! NO!

VZZZ

ALRIGHT! DOUBLE PRIZE!

LET'S GO HOME AND PLAY. HA! HA! HA!

A LITTLE WHILE LATER, WOODY CREEPS OUT OF HIS HIDING PLACE...

BUZZ? THE COAST IS CLEAR.

BUZZ! WHAT HAPPENED TO YOU?

OHHH! I'M A SHAM! LOOK AT ME! I CAN'T EVEN FLY OUT OF A WINDOW!

"OUT OF THE WINDOW!" BUZZ...YOU'RE A GENIUS!

"COME ON! TO SID'S ROOM!"

HEY, GUYS! GUYS!

WOODY! I KNEW YOU'D COME BACK!

WHAT ARE YOU DOING OVER THERE?

IT'S A LONG STORY. HERE, CATCH THIS AND TIE IT TO SOMETHING!

SWISHH

SID!

NOT NOW, MOM, I'M BUSY!

WOODY AND THE OTHERS HIDE, WHILE BUZZ...

IT CAME! IT FINALLY CAME!

"THE BIG ONE," COOL! WHAT AM I GONNA BLOW UP?

THE BIG ONE

YES! I'VE ALWAYS WANTED TO PUT A SPACEMAN INTO ORBIT! HA-HA!

LUCKILY...

SID PHILLIPS REPORTING. LAUNCH OF THE SHUTTLE HAS BEEN DELAYED DUE TO ADVERSE WEATHER CONDITIONS.

TOMORROW'S FORECAST... SUNNY! HA-HA-HA!

RA-BOOM

BAM

OH, NO...

MUCH LATER...

ZZZ

PSSST! HEY, BUZZ! GET OVER HERE AND SEE IF YOU CAN GET THIS TOOLBOX OFF ME!

COME ON, BUZZ. I... I NEED YOUR HELP.

I CAN'T HELP ANYONE...

YOU WERE RIGHT, I'M NOT A SPACE RANGER. I'M JUST A *STUPID* INSIGNIFICANT TOY.

HEY...BEING A TOY IS A *LOT* BETTER THAN BEING A SPACE RANGER!

LOOK, OVER AT THAT HOUSE THERE'S A KID WHO THINKS YOU'RE THE GREATEST BECAUSE YOU'RE *HIS* TOY!

BUT WHY WOULD ANDY WANT *ME*?

WHY?! YOU'RE A BUZZ LIGHTYEAR! YOU'RE A *COOL* TOY!

AS A MATTER OF FACT, YOU'RE *TOO* COOL. WHY WOULD ANDY EVER WANT TO PLAY WITH *ME* WHEN HE'S GOT *YOU*?

WHILE ANDY GETS READY TO LEAVE WITHOUT HIS FAVORITE TOYS...

BUZZ... WOODY...

...AT SID'S HOME, THE RESCUE PLAN GETS UNDER WAY.

FRRR

LEGS AND DUCKY MAKE THEIR WAY TOWARD THE FRONT PORCH AND...

DING DONG

THE SIGNAL! GO!

THE FROG IS LET LOOSE AND *SCUD* CHASES AFTER IT...

ARF

ARF

VRRRROOM

DING DONG

I'M COMING!

...WHILE HANNAH WALKS TO THE FRONT DOOR...

...JUST AT THE RIGHT TIME!

VRRR ROOM

AAH!
CUD!

SBAM

ARF ARF

FRRR

ARF ARF

DUCKY CATCHES THE FROG AND IS QUICKLY REELED UPWARDS...

STUPID DOG!

SLAM

NOW THE COAST IS CLEAR FOR WOODY AND THE OTHERS!

RUUMBLE

...WHILE HANNAH SLAMS THE FRONT DOOR--SCUD HAS BEEN DUPED!

WOOOM

LET'S GO!

HOUSTON! REQUESTING PERMISSION TO LAUNCH... *HEY!*

HOW'D *YOU* GET OUT HERE?

OH, WELL, YOU AND I CAN HAVE A *COOKOUT* LATER. *HA-HA-HA!*

ROCKET LAUNCH IN *THREE! TWO! ONE...*

REACH FOR THE SKY!

WHAT?

THIS TOWN AIN'T BIG ENOUGH FOR THE TWO OF US!

OH, NO! HE'S AT IT *AGAIN!*

CREEEK

WOODY'S ONLY TRYING TO SAVE BUZZ...

?!

VRRROOM

...BUT HIS FRIENDS DON'T KNOW THAT.

TOSS 'IM OVERBOARD!

NO! WAIT! YOU DON'T UNDERSTAND! BUZZ IS OUT THERE...

TUMP

STOMP

TUMP

OH! WOODY!

SLASH

THANKS FOR THE RIDE! NOW, LET'S CATCH UP WITH THAT TRUCK!

GUYS! WOODY'S RIDING RC! AND BUZZ IS WITH HIM!

HE WAS TELLING THE *TRUTH!*

BUT JUST THEN...

OH NO! THE BATTERIES... THEY'VE RUN OUT!

VRRR *SPUT* *SPUT*

WOODY! THE ROCKET!

THE SHERIFF GETS A BRILLIANT IDEA...

HOLD STILL, BUZZ!

FOOM

YOU DID IT! NEXT STOP... *ANDY!*

WAIT A MINUTE...I JUST LIT A *ROCKET.* ROCKETS EXPLO--

SHA-WOOOM

LET RC GO!

LOOK! IT'S WOODY AND BUZZ!

SBAAAM

THIS IS THE PART WHERE WE *BLOW* UP!

NOT TODAY!

CLICK

CLACK

KA-BcoM

TO INFINITY... AND BEYOND!

BUZZ! YOU'RE FLYING!

THIS ISN'T FLYING. THIS IS...FALLING WITH STYLE!

HUH? WE MISSED THE TRUCK!

WE'RE NOT AIMING FOR THE TRUCK!

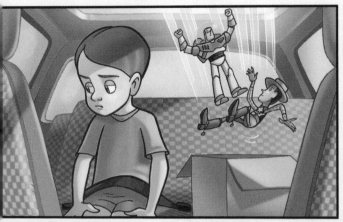

!

WHUMP

WOODY! BUZZ!

OH, GREAT, YOU FOUND THEM. WHERE WERE THEY?

HERE! IN THE CAR!

SEE? NOW, WHAT DID I TELL YOU?

RIGHT WHERE YOU LEFT THEM...

FROM A DISTANCE
ANT ISLAND LOOKS
PEACEFUL AND QUIET,
DOZING UNDER
A LATE SUMMER SUN.

BUT THE ANTS WHO LIVE ON ANT ISLAND ARE
RACING AGAINST TIME, WORKING FRANTICALLY
TO GATHER THEIR ANNUAL OFFERINGS OF
GRAIN FOR THEIR FEARED ENEMIES...

...THE GRASSHOPPERS!

THEY'LL BE
HERE SOON!

ATTA, RELAX. IT'LL BE FINE. IT'S THE SAME EVERY YEAR.
THE GRASSHOPPERS COME, THEY EAT, THEY LEAVE.
THAT'S OUR LOT IN LIFE.

DITCH DOT!

HEY !
COME BACK!!

DOT! WHAT DID I TELL YOU
ABOUT TRYING TO FLY?

NOW, DOT,
YOU'RE A YOUNG
QUEEN ANT, AND
YOUR WINGS ARE
TOO LITTLE--

NOT UNTIL MY
WINGS GROW IN.

BUT MOM--

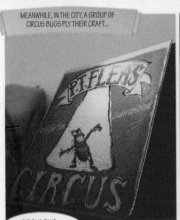

MEANWHILE, IN THE CITY, A GROUP OF CIRCUS BUGS PLY THEIR CRAFT...

P.T. FLEA'S

CIRCUS

CRACK!

BOO!

HISS! BOO!

OW!

I'VE BEEN IN OUTHOUSES THAT DIDN'T STINK THAT BAD!

OOOH! OW! OWIE, OWIE, OWIE!

OH, I'M SO SORRY, DIM! SHOW ROSIE YOUR OWIE.

WE'RE LOSIN' THE AUDIENCE! YOU CLOWNS GET OUT THERE NOW!

I HATE PERFORMING ON AN EMPTY STOMACH!

WHAT'S THE POINT? THEY'LL ONLY LAUGH AT ME!

TRA-LA-LA-LA. I AM A FLOWER...

AND I AM A CUTE LITTLE BUMBLEBEE...

HEY, CUTIE!

COME TO PAPA!

SO BEING A LADYBUG MAKES ME A GIRL-- HUH, FLYBOY!?

CRIPES! SHE'S A GUY!

FLAMING DEATH!

IN A MOMENT, I WILL LIGHT A TRAIL OF MATCHES, LEADING TO A SHEET OF FLYPAPER DOUSED IN LIGHTER FLUID!

AIMED DIRECTLY AT THE FLYPAPER ARE TUCK & ROLL, THE PILLBUG CANNONBALLS. THE CANNON WILL BE TRIGGERED BY DIM...

...TRAINED TO JUMP AT THE SOUND OF THIS BELL, SET TO GO OFF IN 15 SECONDS.

OUR PILLBUGS' ONLY HOPE OF SURVIVAL IS OUR MISTRESS OF THE HIGH WIRE, *ROSIE*, WHO WILL SPIN A WEB TO CATCH THEM-- *BEFORE* THEY HIT THE FLYPAPER.

AND THEY WILL ALL BE... *BLINDFOLDED!*

ALL RIGHT, CLOWN, GET UP AND FIGHT LIKE A GIRL!

SHOO FLY, DON'T BOTHER ME.

GET READY TO DO THE "ROBIN HOOD" BIT.

HUZZAH! STAND *BACK*! *WE* ARE THE GREATEST WARRIORS IN THE SHIRE! LITTLE JOHN?

YA VOL!

FIGHT!

FIGHT!

WARRIOR BUGS! I WANT TO WATCH THIS!

WATCH OUT!

ME THINKETH IT'S NOT WORKING!

BACK TO SHERWOOD FOREST!

RUN!

CRASH

THWACK!

BANG!

THE BUG BAR CAN BEGINS TO LEAN, CREAKING LOOSE FROM ITS FOUNDATION!

THUD!

BANG!

CREEEEEK!

CRASH!

IT ROLLS DOWNHILL....

...AND SLAMS INTO THE SIDE OF THE PORCH RAILING!

CRASH!

OH, GREAT ONES! I HAVE BEEN LOOKING **ALL** OVER FOR TALENT LIKE **YOURS!**

HUH?

WHA-?

A TALENT SCOUT?!

HERE?!

MY COLONY IS IN TROUBLE! GRASSHOPPERS ARE COMING! WE'VE BEEN FORCED TO PREPARE ALL THIS FOOD!

HOW EXCITING! DINNER THEATRE!

YES!

CAN YOU HELP US?

UUUNGH, UUUGH...

THIS IS TOO GOOD TO BE TRUE!

BUT DON'T YOU WANT TO HEAR THE DETAILS?

YES, YES, WE LOVE DETAILS!

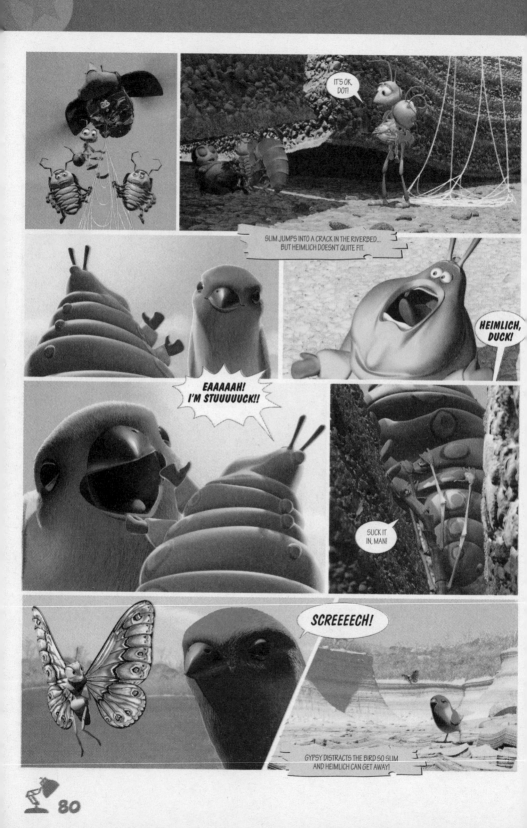

...THE NET BREAKS!

TWANG!

SNAP!

EEIEEIEIEIE!!!

IT LOOKS LIKE THE RESCUERS WILL MAKE IT, WHEN...

HOLD ON, DOT!

AAAIIIEEEE!

SAFE AT LAST, THE BUGS HEAR...

YAY!

BRAVO!

HOORAY!

YAHOO!

BRAVA!

APPLAUSE? I'M IN HEAVEN!

...WE'LL HIDE IT IN THE TREE ABOVE THE ANTHILL. WHEN HOPPER AND HIS GANG ARE BELOW, WE LAUNCH THE BIRD, AND... ...*PRESTO!* BYE BYE, GRASSHOPPERS!

THINKING THAT THE BIRD IS THE CIRCUS BUGS' IDEA, ATTA AND THE COUNCIL AGREE.

I KNOW WE CAN RALLY TOGETHER TO BUILD THIS BIRD!

WITH NEWFOUND HOPE AND COURAGE, THE ANT COLONY GOES TO WORK!

THE CIRCUS BUGS WORK SIDE BY SIDE WITH THE ANTS IN FRIENDLY CAMARADERIE.

AS THE BIRD TAKES SHAPE...

THAT'S IT! GOOD!

... THE CLEARING ECHOES WITH SHOUTS OF LAUGHTER!

AT LAST THE BIRD IS FINISHED!

A CHEER GOES UP! LET THE GRASSHOPPERS COME!

THE ANTS ARE READY FOR THEM!

MEANWHILE, AT THE SOMBRERO BAR...

... IF IT STARTS TO RAIN WHILE WE'RE THERE, WE MIGHT AS WELL SUCK BUG SPRAY.

YEAH. WHY TAKE THE RISK?

GO TELL HOPPER WE WANNA STAY HERE!

THE GUYS AND I HAVE BEEN THINKIN'-- WHY RISK GOING BACK TO ANT ISLAND?

WHAT?!

I DIDN'T THINK IT WAS SUCH A GOOD IDEA. IT WAS AXLE AND LOCO! THEY TALKED ME INTO IT!

I GOT CONFUSED!

GUYS, ORDER ANOTHER ROUND! WE'RE STAYING HERE!

RIGHT ON!

WAY TO GO, MOLT!

COOL!

BUT THERE WAS THAT **ONE** ANT WHO STOOD UP TO ME...

IT WAS JUST ONE PUNY LITTLE ANT, BOSS.

YEAH-- PUNY!

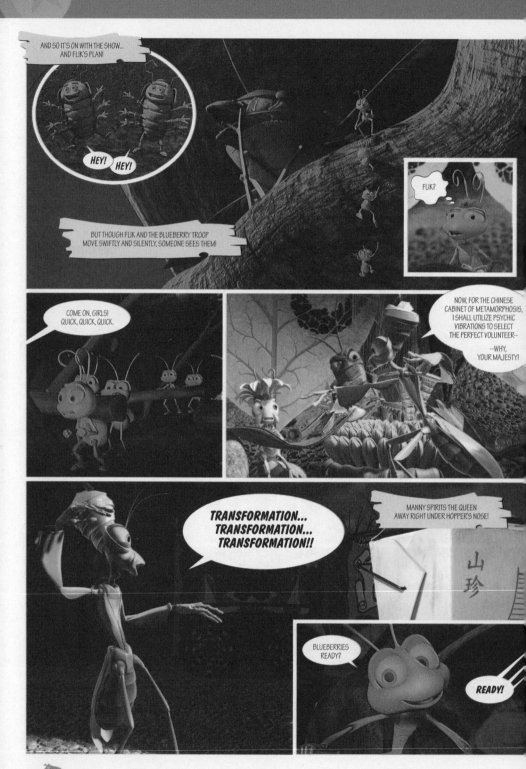

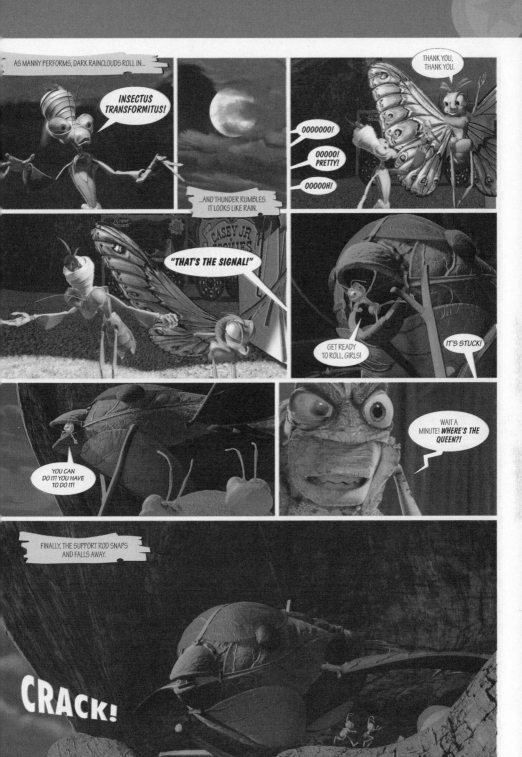

MANNY PRETENDS TO BE DYING...

OH, THE PAIN!

P.T. THINKS THE PERORMANCE IS REAL...

THERE GOES MY MAGIC ACT!

...AND TRIES TO SAVE WHAT'S LEFT OF HIS CIRCUS TROUPE!

FLAMING DEATH!

NO, P.T.!

DIRECT HIT! HA HA!!

THINGS LOOK BAD FOR FLIK!

VALIANTLY, THE CIRCUS BUGS TRY TO RESCUE THEIR FRIEND!

BUT HOPPER IS TOO QUICK!

THE CIRCUS BUGS GET CAUGHT IN THE TREE BRANCHES.

JUST THEN, A BLUR RACES PAST, PULLING FLIK FROM HOPPER'S GRASP. IT'S ATTA!

THANKS, ATTA!

HEAD FOR THE RIVERBED! I HAVE AN IDEA!

HOPPER IS IN PURSUIT...

...WHEN A RAINDROP SLAMS FLIK AND ATTA TO THE GROUND!

SPLAT!

UNH! COME ON--GOTTA HIDE!

NO MATTER WHAT HAPPENS, STAY DOWN! I HAVE A PLAN!

BUT FL--

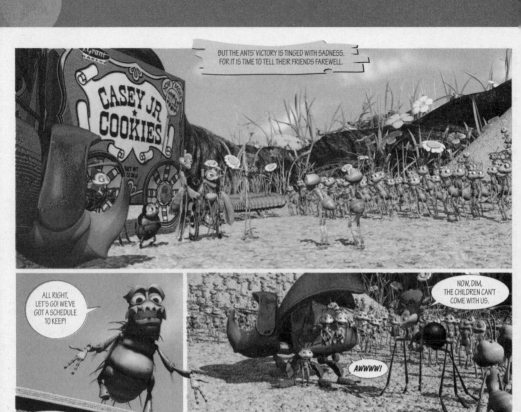

BUT THE ANTS' VICTORY IS TINGED WITH SADNESS. FOR IT IS TIME TO TELL THEIR FRIENDS FAREWELL.

CASEY JR ★ COOKIES

ALL RIGHT, LET'S GO! WE'VE GOT A SCHEDULE TO KEEP!

NOW, DIM, THE CHILDREN CAN'T COME WITH US.

AWWWW!

I'M NOT GONNA CRY. I'M NOT GONNA CRY.

THANK ALL OF YOU FOR GIVING US BACK OUR HOPE, OUR DIGNITY, AND OUR LIVES.

ATTA TOSSES HER TIARA TO DOT, WHO FLIES INTO THE AIR AND CATCHES IT ON HER HEAD!

YIPPEE!

OH! FINALLY, I AM A BEAUTIFUL BUTTERFLY!

FAREWELL, FLIK!

GOOD LUCK!

GOODBYE!

BREAK A LEG!

THORNY AND THE WORKER ANTS LINE UP IN FORMATION WEARING FLIK'S HARVESTERS.

PRESENT STALKS! HARVESTER... *SALUTE!*

YOU'RE NEVER GOING TO LET ME FORGET THIS, ARE YOU?

WHATEVER MADE YOU THINK CIRCUS BUGS WERE WARRIORS?

NOT A CHANCE!

AT LONG LAST, PEACE AND PROSPERITY HAVE SETTLED ON ANT ISLAND AND ITS TINY, COURAGEOUS INHABITANTS.

THE END

...LOOKING FOR A HAT!

ANDY'S LEAVING FOR **COWBOY CAMP** AND I CAN'T FIND IT **ANYWHERE!**

WOODY, LOOK UNDER YOUR **BOOT.**

MY HAT IS **NOT** UNDER MY BOOT, **BO.** THERE'S ONLY THE WORD **ANDY!**

AND THE BOY WHO WROTE THAT WOULD TAKE YOU TO CAMP, WITH OR **WITHOUT** YOUR HAT!

GOOD NEWS, I FOUND YOUR HAT, WOODY!

AW, SLINKY... THANK YOU!

EVERYTHING IS BACK TO NORMAL AND BEFORE LEAVING, ANDY PLAYS WITH HIS TOYS ONCE MORE...

LET HER GO, EVIL DR. PORK CHOP!

NEVER! YOU MUST CHOOSE, SHERIFF WOODY...

107

HOW SHALL SHE DIE? SHARK?

OR DEATH BY MONKEYS?

I CHOOSE... BUZZ LIGHTYEAR!

CLIC

TO INFINITY AND BEYOND!

VRRROOM

BAM

THANKS, BUZZ!

NO PROBLEM, BUDDY! YOU SHOULD NEVER TANGLE WITH THE UNSTOPPABLE DUO OF WOODY AND BUZZ LIGHTYEAR!

RIP

OH, NO...

ANDY, LET'S GO. THE CAMP IS WAITING.

BUT MOM, WOODY'S ARM **RIPPED**.

I'M SORRY, HONEY, BUT YOU KNOW, **TOYS DON'T LAST FOREVER.**

FOR THE FIRST TIME, ANDY GOES TO COWBOY CAMP WITHOUT HIS FAVORITE TOY.

AND FOR THE FIRST TIME, THAT TOY FEELS REALLY SAD AND LONELY...

WHAT HAPPENED?

WOODY'S BEEN **SHELVED!**

109

HE'S SELLING HIMSELF FOR 25 CENTS!

HOLD ON, HOLD ON, HE'S GOT SOMETHING... IT'S **WHEEZY**!

IT'S NOT **SUICIDE**, IT'S A **RESCUE**!

BUT EVERY RESCUE HAS ITS INCONVENIENCES...

NOW... BACK TO ANDY'S **ROO-OOF**!

NO, NO, NO...

MOMMY! LOOK AT THIS! IT'S A COWBOY DOLLY...

ZRRR

OH, HONEY, WE'RE NOT BUYING ANY **BROKEN** TOYS.

THERE'S A SNAKE IN MY BOOT.

!

ORIGINAL HAND PAINTED FACE, NATURAL DYED BLANKET-STITCHED VEST...I FOUND HIM! I FOUND HIM!

HEY! WHAT'S HE DOING?

OH NO... HE'S STEALING WOODY!

SOMEBODY DO SOMETHING!

LIKE A TRUE SPACE RANGER, BUZZ RACES TO HELP HIS FRIEND...

SHOOM!

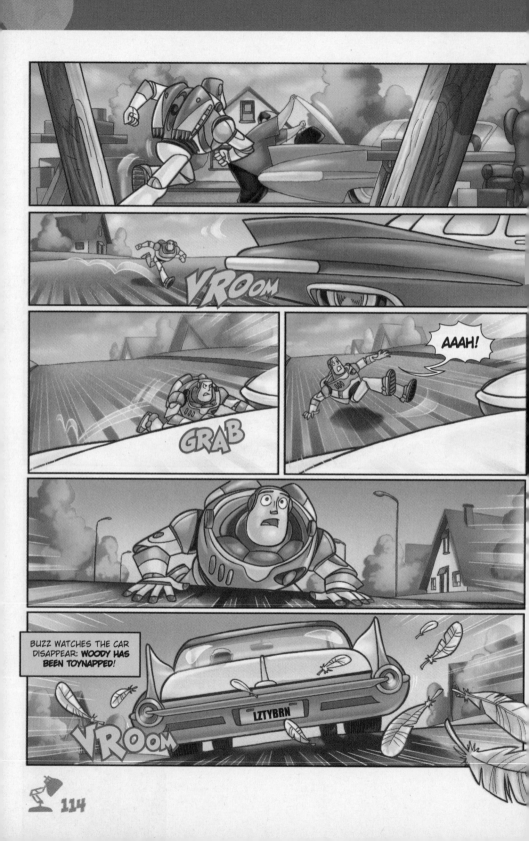

FAR FROM THERE...

YOU, MY LITTLE COWBOY FRIEND, ARE GOING TO MAKE ME BIG...

...BUCK, BUCK, **BUCKS!** **HAHAHA!**

SLAM

AL LEAVES...

...DRIVING TO HIS STORE ACROSS THE STREET...

VRCOOOM

...AND WOODY IS FINALLY FREE TO ESCAPE.

ISN'T HE?

FRUSH

WHAT...

116

PROSPECTOR SAID SOME DAY YOU'D COME! HE'LL WANNA MEETCHA!

"HE'S MINT IN THE BOX. NEVER BEEN OPENED."

WE'VE WAITED COUNTLESS YEARS FOR THIS DAY...

...IT'S GOOD TO SEE YOU, WOODY!

HEY, HOW DO YOU KNOW MY NAME?

YOU DON'T KNOW WHO YOU ARE, DO YOU?

BULLSEYE! TURN ON THE LIGHTS...

CLICK

HOLY COW!

BUT THE NEXT MORNING AL CALLS A TOY-CLEANER TO FIX WOODY'S ARM...

...AND ERASES HIS PAST.

MY WORK IS DONE.

YOU'RE A GENIUS! HE'S JUST LIKE **NEW!**

HIS FRIENDS MUST RUSH IF THEY WANT TO SAVE HIM...

HURRAY! THE **CHICKEN!**

WE MADE IT.

THEY'RE IN FRONT OF AL'S TOY BARN, BUT THERE'S ONE LITTLE PROBLEM...

AL'S TOY BARN

VROOOM

!!!

...HOW DO THEY GET ACROSS THE STREET?

IN THE MEANTIME, AL IS TAKING PICTURES OF HIS PRECIOUS NEW TOY...

...FOR HIS COLLECTION BUYER FROM JAPAN.

MR. KONISHI, I HAVE THE **PICTURES** RIGHT HERE!

I'M ON MY WAY TO THE **OFFICE** TO **FAX** THEM TO YOU!

OH, WOW! LOOK AT THIS STITCHING! ANDY'S GONNA HAVE A HARD TIME RIPPING THIS!

GREAT, **NOW** YOU CAN **GO!**

WOODY, DON'T BE MAD AT **JESSIE**. SHE'S BEEN THROUGH MORE THAN YOU KNOW. WHY NOT MAKE AMENDS BEFORE YOU LEAVE, HUH?

"IT'S THE LEAST YOU CAN DO."

HEY! WHATCHA DOING WAY UP, THERE?

I THOUGHT I'D GET ONE LAST LOOK AT THE SUN, BEFORE I GET **PACKED AWAY** AGAIN.

LOOK, JESSIE, I'M SORRY, BUT I'VE TO GO BACK. I'M STILL **ANDY'S TOY.** IF YOU KNEW HIM YOU'D UNDERSTAND. HE'S--

LET ME GUESS. ANDY'S A REAL **SPECIAL** KID AND YOU'RE HIS **BUDDY** AND WHEN ANDY PLAYS WITH YOU, IT'S LIKE...

...EVEN THOUGH YOU'RE **NOT MOVING,** YOU FEEL LIKE YOU'RE **ALIVE.**

BECAUSE THAT'S HOW HE SEES YOU.

HOW DID YOU **KNOW** THAT?

BECAUSE **EMILY** WAS JUST THE SAME.

"SHE WAS MY **WHOLE WORLD.**"

"WE HAD EACH OTHER AND THAT WAS **ENOUGH.**"

"BUT SHE BEGAN TO **GROW UP,** AND I WAS LEFT UNDER THE BED, **ALONE.**"

"UNTIL ONE DAY..."

"...SHE **GAVE ME AWAY.**"

WOODY MADE HIS DECISION... BUT SOMEONE WOULD NOT BE HAPPY TO HEAR THAT!

WOODY? ARE YOU HERE?

YOU SEE, THE SECRET ENTRANCE TO ZURG'S FORTRESS IS TO THE LEFT, IN THE SHADOWS!

LEFT. SHADOWS. GOT IT.

CLACK

SHH... SOMEONE'S COMING!

LET ME CONFIRM YOUR FAX NUMBER... I PROMISE THE COLLECTION WITH **WOODY** AND THE **ROUNDUP** WILL BE THE CROWN JEWEL OF YOUR MUSEUM!

THAT'S THE **KIDNAPPER**!

AN AGENT OF ZURG!

OH YES! WE'VE GOT A DEAL! I'LL BE ON THE NEXT FLIGHT TO JAPAN!

QUICK! INTO THE POULTRY MAN'S CARGO UNIT. HE'LL LEAD US TO ZURG!

ON THE OTHER SIDE OF THE STREET, AL WALKS TOWARDS HIS APARTMENT...

...LEAVING HIS BAG BEHIND!

LET'S GO!

HE'S ASCENDING IN THE **VERTICAL TRANSPORTER**!

OH, NO! HOW ARE WE GONNA GET UP THERE?

TROOPS! **OVER HERE!**

JUST LIKE YOU SAID, LIZARD MAN. IN THE **SHADOWS**, TO THE **LEFT!** LET'S MOVE!

STOCK

AHHHH!

CRASH

BUZZ! GUYS! HOW DID YOU FIND ME?

WE'RE HERE TO SPRING YOU!

YOU HEARD OF KUNG FU? WELL, GET READY FOR **PORK CHOP!**

BUMP

GRAB WOODY AND LET'S GO!

CLINK

IN A MINUTE THEY WILL BE GONE AND A WHOLE NEW LIFE WILL START FOR WOODY...

...A LIFE WATCHING KIDS FROM BEHIND A GLASS, BEING LOVED NO MORE.

WHAT AM I DOING?

BUZZ! WAIT! I'M COMING WITH **YOU!**

WOODY?

COME WITH ME, GUYS! ANDY WILL **PLAY** WITH **ALL OF US!**

WHAT? I...I DON'T KNOW...

WOULDN'T YOU GIVE ANYTHING JUST TO HAVE **ONE MORE DAY** WITH EMILY?

NO!

CLANG

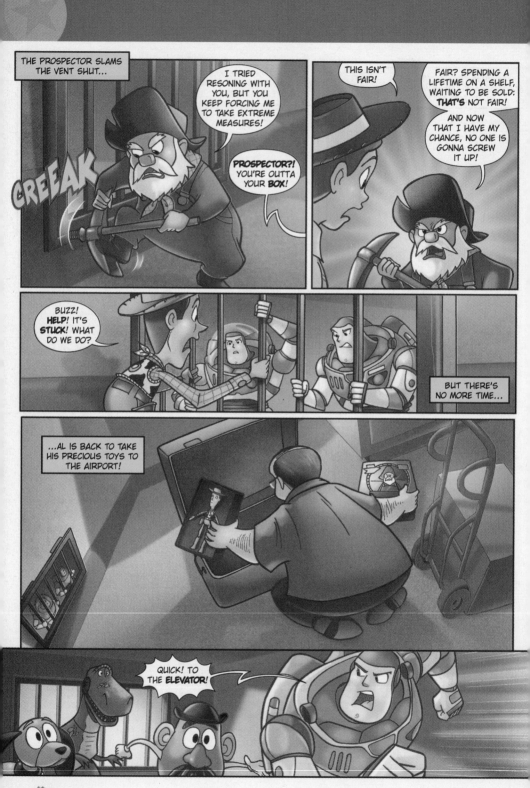

OH, NO!

HOW ARE WE GONNA GET HIM NOW?

VROOM

PIZZA, ANYONE?

YO

THERE'S NO TIME TO LOSE! HOWEVER, THE NEW BUZZ ISN'T COMING.

GO LONG, BUZZY!

YOU'RE A GREAT DAD!

HIS DAD ZURG SURVIVED THE FALL. THE TWO OF THEM HAVE A LOT TO DO TOGETHER NOW!

VRRROOM

FAR EAST

CLOP CLOP CLOP

CLOP CLOP CLOP

GRAB

WHOA!

FAR EAST

FAR EAST

SCREEE

WHILE THE SUITCASE IS BEING LOADED ONTO THE PLANE...

ZZZZZZ

...WOODY IS NOT FAR!

148

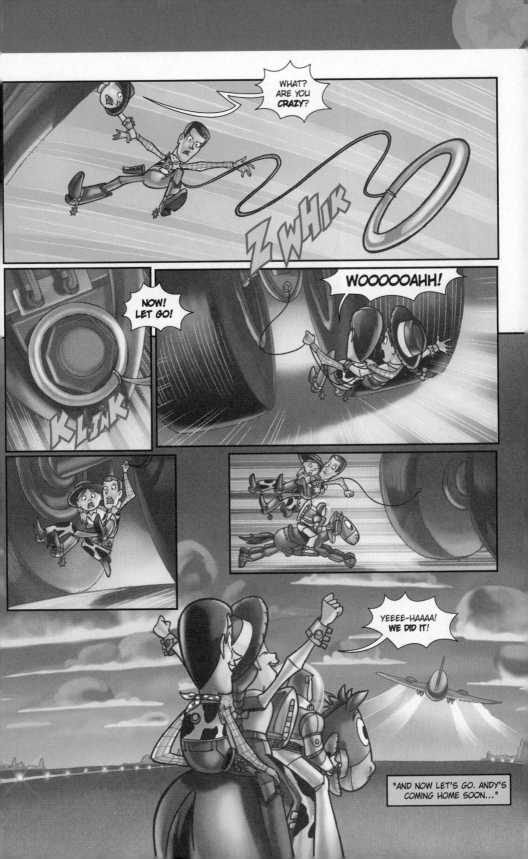

BACK TO ANDY'S ROOM...

OH, WOW!

NEW TOYS-- **COOL!**

WELCOME Home ANDY

AND THE NEXT DAY...

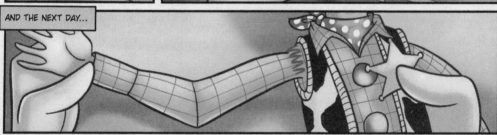

COME ON, HON. TIME TO GO. HEY, YOU **FIXED** WOODY!

YEAH. GOOD THING I DIDN'T BRING HIM TO COWBOY CAMP. HIS WHOLE ARM MIGHT'VE COME OFF.

SLAM

WELL, WHAT DO YOU KNOW?

SIMULATION TERMINATED! SIMULATION TERMINATED!

WHIIRRRR

MR. BILE, YOU LEFT THE DOOR WIDE OPEN. AND THAT IS THE WORST MISTAKE ANY EMPLOYEE CAN MAKE BECAUSE ....

...IT COULD LET IN A CHILD!

GASP!

OH, MR. WATERNOOSE!

AAAAGHHH!

THERE IS *NOTHING* MORE TOXIC THAN A HUMAN CHILD! A *SINGLE* TOUCH COULD KILL YOU! IT'S DANGEROUS WORK, BUT OUR CITY IS *COUNTING* ON YOU TO COLLECT THOSE CHILDREN'S *SCREAMS.*

WITHOUT SCREAMS, WE HAVE NO POWER! I NEED SCARERS WHO ARE CONFIDENT...TOUGH... INTIMIDATING, LIKE...

"...LIKE JAMES P. SULLIVAN!"

ZZZZZZZZ

GET UP, SULLEY! WORKOUT TIME!

BLAAAAT

157

THE NEXT MORNING, AT THE BOYS' APARTMENT, MIKE COACHES SULLEY THROUGH HIS EXERCISE ROUTINE...

LET'S HIT IT.

WORK IT! WORK IT! YOU'RE NUMBER ONE 'CAUSE YOU GET THE JOB DONE!

FEEL THE BURN!

READY? BUNK BEDS!

GRRR!

GRRR!

GRRRRR

SCARY FEET! SCARY FEET! SCARY FEET!

I DUNNO BUT IT'S BEEN SAID, I LOVE SCARING KIDS IN BED.

GRRRRR

FIGHT THAT PLAQUE! SCARY MONSTERS DON'T HAVE PLAQUE!

118...119...120. I DON'T BELIEVE IT!

I'M NOT EVEN BREAKING A SWEAT.

THE NEW COMMERCIAL'S ON!

THE FUTURE IS BRIGHT AT MONSTERS INCORPORATED!

I'M IN THIS ONE! I'M IN THIS ONE!

WE POWER YOUR CAR...WE WARM YOUR HOME...WE LIGHT YOUR CITY.

EEEEEEE!

CAREFULLY MATCHING EVERY CHILD TO THEIR IDEAL MONSTER...

TO PRODUCE SUPERIOR SCREAM REFINED INTO CLEAN, DEPENDABLE ENERGY...

WE KNOW THE CHALLENGE. THE WINDOW OF INNOCENCE IS SHRINKING. HUMAN KIDS ARE HARDER TO SCARE.

M.I. IS PREPARED FOR THE FUTURE, WITH THE TOP SCARERS, THE BEST REFINERIES AND RESEARCH INTO NEW ENERGY TECHNIQUES.

RAAAAAAAHR!

OK, HERE I COME!

MONSTERS, INCORPORATED. WE SCARE...BECAUSE WE CARE.

I CAN'T BELIEVE IT...

OH, MIKE.

I WAS ON TV! I'M A NATURAL. THE CAMERA LOVES ME!

IT'S A TYPICAL MORNING IN MONSTROPOLIS...

I'M TELLING YOU, YOU'RE GOING TO BE SEEING THIS FACE ON TV A LOT!

YEAH? LIKE ON MONSTROPOLIS'S MOST WANTED?

NOPE. UH-UH.

HOP ON IN!

HEY, WHERE ARE YOU GOING?! WHAT ARE YOU DOING?!

MIKEY, THERE'S A SCREAM SHORTAGE. WE'RE WALKING.

HEY GENIUS, KNOW WHY I BOUGHT THE CAR? TO DRIVE IT!

GIVE IT A REST, BUTTERBALL. YOU COULD USE THE EXERCISE.

MORNING, MIKE! MORNING, SULLEY!

HEY, KIDS!

HEY SULLEY, I HEAR YOU'RE CLOSE TO BREAKING THE ALL-TIME SCARE RECORD.

JUST TRYING TO MAKE SURE THERE'S ENOUGH SCREAM TO GO AROUND.

SEE THAT, MIKEY? TED'S WALKING TO WORK.

BIG DEAL! GUY TAKES FIVE STEPS AND HE'S THERE.

STALK DON'T STALK

'MORNING, SULLEY.

IT'S THE SULLSTER!

HOW YA DOING, BIG GUY!

GOOD LUCK, MR. SULLIVAN

OH, SORRY!

HEY, GET LOST. YOU'RE MAKING HIM LOSE HIS FOCUS.

MONSTERS, INC., PLEASE HOLD. MONSTERS INC., I'LL CONNECT YOU.

OH SHMOOPSIE-POO...HAPPY BIRTHDAY! TONIGHT WE'RE GOING TO A LITTLE PLACE CALLED, UM...HARRY HAUSEN'S.

BUT IT'S IMPOSSIBLE TO GET A RESERVATION THERE!

AHHHH!

I'LL SEE YOU AT 5:01. THINK ROMANTICAL THOUGHTS!

YOU KNOW PAL, SHE'S THE ONE! SHE IS THE ONE!

I'M HAPPY FOR YA.

BANG

GASP!

WHATTAYA KNOW...IT SCARES LITTLE KIDS AND LITTLE MONSTERS!

UH...I WASN'T SCARED. I HAVE... ALLERGIES.

HEY, RANDALL, SAVE IT FOR THE SCARE FLOOR, WILL YA?

I'M IN THE ZONE TODAY SULLIVAN. GOING TO BE DOING SOME SERIOUS SCARING, PUTTING UP SOME BIG NUMBERS.

WHAT A CREEP! ONE OF THESE DAYS I AM GOING TO LET YOU TEACH THAT GUY A LESSON.

GOOD MORNING, ROZ, MY LITTLE GARDEN SNAIL, AND WHO WILL WE BE SCARING TODAY?

WAZOWSKI. YOU DIDN'T FILE YOUR PAPERWORK LAST NIGHT.

DON'T LET IT HAPPEN AGAIN.

YES! WELL, I'LL TRY TO BE LESS CARELESS.

I'M WATCHING YOU WAZOWKSI, *ALWAYS* WATCHING.

ALL SCARE FLOORS ARE NOW ACTIVE. ASSISTANTS, PLEASE REPORT TO YOUR STATIONS.

OOOH, SHE'S NUTS!

ALL ACROSS THE SCARE FLOOR, THE ASSISTANTS PREPARE CANS TO CAPTURE SCREAM ENERGY...

...AND CALL UP THE DOORS TO SLEEPING KIDS' BEDROOMS AROUND THE WORLD.

WHHHHHIR

THUNKTHUNKTHUNKTHUNKTHUN

EASTERN SEABOARD COMING ONLINE. WE GOT SCARERS, COMING OUT.

LIKE TOP ATHLETES, THE SCARERS READY THEMSELVES.

SNAP! SNAP! SNAP! SNAP! SNAP!

CRRRACK!

PLOP PLOP PLOP

RANDALL, SULLIVAN'S RIVAL, PRACTICES HIS CAMOFLAGE SKILLS.

SCARE TOTALS

SULLIVAN 99,479

RANDALL 99,351

HEY, MAY THE BEST MONSTER WIN.

I PLAN TO.

WE ARE ON IN SEVEN... SIX...

FIVE...FOUR...THREE...TWO...

YOU'RE THE BOSS, YOU'RE THE BIG HAIRY BOSS!

...SCARE!

EEEEEEE AAAAAAAAAAA MMMMMAAAA

YEAH! I'M FEELING GOOD TODAY, MIKEY!

THAT A BOY! ANOTHER DOOR COMIN' RIGHT UP!

YOU'RE STILL BEHIND, RANDALL.

GRRRRRRRR! JUST GET ME ANOTHER DOOR!

EEEEEEE AAAAAI\\\\. MAAAAAAAMA

SULLIVAN	99,479
RANDALL	
RANFT	99,351
LUCKEY	79,012
RIVERA	68,245
PETERSON	67,992
JONES	
SANDERSON	67,236
PLESUSKI	66,101
	58,986
SCHMIDT	55,735
PAULEY	
WARD	44,421
GERSON	41,918

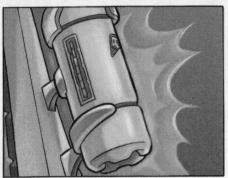

WE MAY MAKE OUR QUOTA TODAY, MR. WATERNOOSE, SIR.

FIRST TIME IN A MONTH.

UH...UH...UH...THE KID ALMOST TOUCHED ME!

SHE WASN'T SCARED OF YOU? SHE WAS ONLY SIX!

I COULD'VE BEEN DEAD! I COULD'VE DIED!

KEEP IT TOGETHER, MAN.

HEY, WE GOT A DEAD DOOR, HERE!

LOOK OUT! DOOR SHREDDER COMING THROUGH!

WE'VE LOST 58 DOORS THIS WEEK, SIR.

KIDS THESE DAYS. THEY JUST DON'T GET *SCARED* LIKE THEY USED TO.

SCREE EEEECH

ATTENTION! WE HAVE A NEW SCARE LEADER: RANDALL BOGGS!

EEEE! EEEE! EEEE!

NICE JOB! YOU TOOK THE LEAD!

LOOK AT THOSE NUMBERS!

YOU DID IT!

SLUMBER PARTY. HEH-HEH!

NEVER MIND.

WHOA!

THAT WAS AWESOME! YOU'RE GOING TO THE HALL OF FAME FOR SURE.

SULLIVAN 100,021

RANDALL 99,851

RANFT 79,061

CURREY

RIVERA

WELL, JAMES, THAT WAS AN IMPRESSIVE DISPLAY.

OF COUSE, I LEARNED FROM THE *BEST*.

IF I DON'T SEE A NEW DOOR IN *FIVE SECONDS*, I WILL PERSONALLY PUT YOU THROUGH THE *SHREDDER*!

AAAAH!

SUDDENLY, DISASTER STRIKES!

KEEP THE DOORS COMIN'. I'M ON A ROLL TODAY.

TWENTY-THREE NINETEEN! WE HAVE A TWENTY-THREE NINETEEN!

RED ALERT, RED ALERT

EMERGENCY

GEORGE SANDERSON, PLEASE REMAIN MOTIONLESS! PREPARE FOR DECONTAMINATION!

GET IT OFF!

DUCK AND COVER, PEOPLE!

ALERTED TO THE DISASTER, THE DREADED C.D.A. (CHILD DETECTIVE AGENCY) RUSHES TO THE SCENE!

COMING THROUGH! CLEAR THE CONTAMINATED AREA! TWENTY-THREE NINETEEN IN PROGRESS!

OOF!

BOOOM

WHA?

AAAAAAH!!

ZZZZZZZZZZZZZZZZ

THE CDA DECONTAMINATES POOR GEORGE...

...RIGHT DOWN TO THE SKIN!

TAKE A BREAK EVERYONE... WE GOTTA SHUT DOWN AND RESET THE SYSTEM.

AN ENTIRE SCARE FLOOR OUT OF COMMISSION. WHAT ELSE CAN GO WRONG?

ACCIDENT FREE FOR 0 DAYS

ANOTHER WORK DAY COMES TO AN END...

LET'S GO. ALL DOORS MUST BE RETURNED. NO EXCEPTIONS!

ANOTHER DAY LIKE THIS AND THAT SCARE RECORD'S IN THE BAG.

YEAH, AND WHAT A NIGHT OF ROMANCE I'VE GOT AHEAD OF ME!

HELLO, WAZOWSKI. FUN-FILLED EVENING PLANNED? AND I'M SURE YOU FILED YOUR PAPERWORK CORRECTLY. FOR ONCE.

EEP! MY SCARE REPORTS! I LEFT THEM ON MY DESK! IF I'M NOT AT THE RESTAURANT IN FIVE MINUTES THEY'LL GIVE MY TABLE AWAY!

HEY, GOGGLEY BEAR! WANT TO GET GOING?

OH, DO I EVER...IT'S JUST THAT... UH...

IT'S JUST THAT I FORGOT ABOUT SOME PAPERWORK. MIKE WAS REMINDING ME. THANKS, BUDDY.

OH! YEAH! WELL... WE'RE OFF!

BUT WHEN SULLEY RETURNS TO THE SCARE FLOOR...

HUH? HELLO? ANYONE? THERE'S AN ACTIVE DOOR HERE.

PSSST! IS ANYBODY SCARING IN HERE? HMM...

THUMP

BABAWADA?

AAAAAAAAAAH!!

SULLIVAN TRIES TO PLACE THE CHILD BACK IN HER ROOM...

AYHA!

AAAAAHH!

BUT SHE SNEAKS OUT AGAIN!

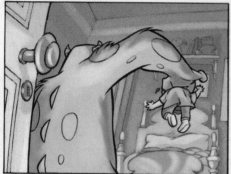

THUD

CRASH

AAAAAHH!

JUST THEN, SULLEY HEARS A NOISE! SOMEONE'S COMING!

SQUEAK

SQUEAK

SQUEAK

SQUEAK

IT'S RANDALL, ON A MYSTERIOUS ERRAND!

WHEW!

KITTY!

WHEN SULLEY RETURNS TO THE SCARE FLOOR...

UH-OH!

RATTLE

RANDALL EJECTS THE CHILD'S DOOR AND LEAVES, WITHOUT SPOTTING SULLEY!

SNIGALALA?

SSSSH!

WITHOUT THE DOOR KEY, SULLIVAN HAS NO WAY TO PUT THE CHILD BACK WHERE SHE BELONGS!

AAAAAH!

HE NEEDS HELP--AND FAST!

MEANWHILE, AT HARRY HAUSEN'S...

OH, MICHAEL, THIS IS THE BEST BIRTHDAY *EVER.*

SOMEONE ASKED ME WHO WAS THE MOST BEAUTIFUL MONSTER IN MONSTROPOLIS. KNOW WHAT I SAID?

SULLEY?

SULLEY?!

HI, GUYS! WHAT A COINCIDENCE, RUNNING INTO YOU HERE!

OOF!

OOK-LAY IN THE AG-BAY!

WHAT?

LOOK IN THE BAG!

WHAT BAG?

HUMPH.

GASP!

UH, THEY DON'T HAVE ANYTHING I LIKE HERE. BYE, CELIA!

CELIA, PLEASE TRY TO UNDERSTAND. I HAVE TO *DO SOMETHING!*

ON THREE. ONE, TWO...*AAAHHH!!*

BOO!

AAAHHH!! A KID!!

HELP!

LET ME OUT!

THERE'S A KID HERE! A HUMAN KID!!

THUD

CRASH

COME ON!

THE CDA ARRIVES IN SECONDS!

WE HAVE AN 835 IN PROGRESS. STAND CLEAR, PLEASE!

MICHAEL! MICHAEL!!

COME WITH US PLEASE, MISS.

WELL, I DON'T THINK THAT DATE COULD HAVE GONE ANY *WORSE!*

BOOOOMMM

CHAOS REIGNS THROUGHOUT MONSTROPOLIS...

KID-TASTROPHY!

...AND IN MIKE AND SULLEY'S APARTMENT!

UH, OH!

CRASH

IT'S ALL RIGHT! AS LONG AS IT DOESN'T COME NEAR US, WE'RE GONNA BE OK.

AA ACHOOO!

AAAH!

FSSS

AAAAHH!

EEEEEEH.

WABBADABGI.

OH, HERE! YOU LIKE THIS?

HEY! NO ONE TOUCHES LITTLE MIKEY!

THE CHILD'S SCREAMS LIGHT UP THE APARTMENT!

EEEEEEEE!

MAKE IT STOP! MAKE IT STOP!

OH, HE'S A HAPPY BEAR...

~SNIFFLE~

EEEEE!

WHEW! GOOD! KEEP IT UP, SULLEY.

SULLEY, THE BEAR! THE BEAR! GIVE IT THE--

WHOOOOOAH!

HEE-HEE-HEE!

THUD

OOF!

THIS TIME HER LAUGHTER MAKES THE ENTIRE BUILDING LIGHT UP!

POP

CRASH

CRASH

CRASH

POP

WHAT WAS *THAT?*

I HAVE NO IDEA, BUT IT WOULD BE REALLY GREAT IF IT DIDN'T DO IT AGAIN.

175

I'M OUT OF IDEAS. HOT AIR BALLOONS... TOO EXPENSIVE. GIANT SLINGSHOT...TOO CONSPICUOUS. ENORMOUS WOODEN HORSE...TOO GREEK.

UH, MIKE, I THINK SHE'S GETTING TIRED.

WELL THEN, FIND SOME PLACE FOR IT TO SLEEP WHILE I THINK OF A PLAN.

OK, I'M MAKING A NICE LITTLE... HEY, THAT'S *MY* BED! AH, FINE...

JABBAKUWA?

IT'S JUST A CLOSET. GO TO SLEEP.

HEY, THAT'S RANDALL. *HE'S* YOUR MONSTER? YOU THINK HE'S GONNA COME THROUGH THE CLOSET?

IT'S *EMPTY,* SEE? NO MONSTERS IN HERE.

GJADAKALAGY?

OK, HOW 'BOUT I SIT HERE UNTIL YOU FALL ASLEEP?

AS HE WATCHES THE SLEEPING CHILD, SOMETHING IN SULLIVAN'S HEART IS TOUCHED.

SIGH.

176

MIKE, I DON'T THINK THAT KID'S DANGEROUS. WHAT IF WE JUST PUT HER BACK IN HER DOOR LIKE IT NEVER HAPPENED?

OH, MARCH OUT INTO PUBLIC AND RIGHT UP TO THE FACTORY?

THIS IS CRAZY. JUST THINK ABOUT A FEW NAMES WILL YA? LOCH NESS, BIG FOOT, THE ABOMINABLE SNOWMAN...THEY ALL GOT ONE THING IN COMMON, PAL-- BANISHMENT!

DON'T PANIC.

DON'T TELL ME NOT TO PANIC! THIS IS NOT OK!

SUDDENLY, THE CHILD GETS AWAY FROM SULLEY AND WALKS UP TO MR. WATERNOOSE!

BOO!

NO, NOT NOW, NOT NOW... I'M...

JAMES! IS THIS ONE YOURS?

ACTUALLY THAT'S MY COUSIN'S SISTER'S...UH, DAUGHTER, SIR.

YEAH, I-IT'S "BRING AN OBSCURE RELATIVE TO WORK DAY."

WAIT HERE, WHILE I GET ITS DOOR KEY CARD.

BUT SHE CAN'T STAY HERE. THIS IS THE MEN'S ROOM.

ROZ, RANDALL WAS WORKING LATE LAST NIGHT ON THE SCARE FLOOR. I REALLY NEED THE KEY FOR THE DOOR HE WAS USING.

YOU DIDN'T TURN IN YOUR PAPERWORK LAST NIGHT. THIS OFFICE IS CLOSED.

AAAAAH

WAAA

JUST AFTER MIKE RETURNS, THE CHILD SEES RANDALL APPEAR!

WHAT'S THE MATTER?

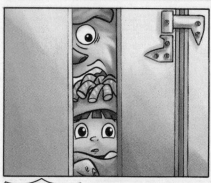

THE CHILD! THE ONE YOU WERE AFTER! WHAT ARE WE GOING TO DO?

YOU JUST GET THE MACHINE RUNNING, *I'LL* TAKE CARE OF THE KID, AND WHEN I FIND WHOEVER LET IT OUT... THEY'RE *DEAD!* GO! MOVE! *NOW!*

DON'T PANIC. WE'LL JUST CALL HER DOOR DOWN AND SEND HER HOME. YOU GOT HER KEY, RIGHT?

I TOLD YOU I'D GET HER CARD KEY. I HAVE HER CARD KEY...

THAT'S NOT *BOO'S* DOOR.

BOO? WHAT'S *BOO*?

THAT'S WHAT I DECIDED TO CALL HER.

YOU'RE NOT SUPPOSED TO *NAME* IT! ONCE YOU NAME IT, YOU START GETTING ATTACHED TO IT! NOW PUT THAT THING BACK WHERE IT CAME FROM OR SO HELP ME--

OH! HEY, WE'RE REHEARSING A SCENE FOR THE UPCOMING COMPANY PLAY, CALLED, "PUT THAT THING BACK WHERE IT CAME FROM OR SO HELP ME...!" IT'S A MUSICAL!

I DON'T BELIEVE IT--SHE GOT AWAY FROM YOU AGAIN! WAIT A MINUTE. THE SUN IS COMING UP... THIS IS PERFECT. HA, HA! SHE'S GONE!

BOO?!

SULLEY, DON'T BLOW THIS! NOT WHEN WE'RE SO CLOSE TO BREAKING THE RECORD. SOMEBODY ELSE WILL FIND THE KID, IT'LL BE THEIR PROBLEM...

WHA--?

WHAT DO YOU THINK OF THAT KID GETTING OUT? PRETTY CRAZY, HUH?

YOU HAVEN'T *SEEN* ANYTHING *HAVE* YOU?

UH... NO...

NO WAY! BUT IF IT WAS AN INSIDE JOB, I'D PUT MY MONEY ON WAXFORD. THE ONE WITH THE SHIFTY EYES.

HEY, WAXFORD! WHAT TIME DID YOU LEAVE LAST NIGHT?

SULLEY!

MICHAEL WAZOWSKI!

LAST NIGHT WAS ONE OF THE *WORST* NIGHTS OF MY *ENTIRE* LIFE!

HISSSS

OH!

SMACK

WAZOWSKI! HMMMM.

MOTHER WAS RIGHT!

WOOOOM

YIKES!

WHERE'S THE KID? IT'S HERE IN THE FACTORY, ISN'T IT?

YES. ER... NO...IT NEVER WOULD HAVE GOTTEN OUT IF YOU HADN'T BEEN CHEATING LAST NIGHT.

WHEN THE BIG HAND POINTS UP AND THE LITTLE HAND POINTS DOWN, THE KID'S DOOR WILL BE IN MY STATION. BUT WHEN THE BIG HAND POINTS DOWN, THE DOOR WILL BE GONE. YOU HAVE UNTIL THEN TO PUT THE KID BACK. GET THE PICTURE?

OOOH.

BOO!

YOU'RE THE ONE FROM THE COMMERCIAL.

HUH?!

CAN WE GET AN AUTOGRAPH?

GASP!

HUH? MIKE, WHERE ARE YA? YOU IN THERE?

GADJAMAWAP.

CLUNK

HUH?

ABODA GABI DU WADO!

AT THE END OF A LONG CORRIDOR...

I GOT THE KID. LET'S GET STARTED.

TH-THAT'S GREAT NEWS. N-NOT THAT I WAS CONCERNED, OF COURSE...

WAZOWSKI!

KIDNAPPING ME ISN'T GONNA HELP YOU CHEAT YOUR WAY TO THE TOP!

YOU STILL THINK THIS IS ABOUT THAT STUPID SCARE RECORD.

WELL, I DID. NOW I'M THINKING I SHOULD JUST GET OUT OF HERE!

VRRRRRRR

I'M ABOUT TO REVOLUTIONIZE THE SCARING INDUSTRY. AND WHEN I DO, EVEN THE GREAT JAMES P. SULLIVAN IS GONNA BE WORKING FOR ME. NOW, TELL ME WHERE THE KID IS.

I DON'T KNOW ANY-THING!

NO, WAIT! HELP! HELP!

WHIRRRRRRRR

PING

SNAP

CLUNK

HMMMMMMMM

YEERP!

WHERE'S WAZOWSKI?

AAAAAH!

WHERE IS HE?

AAAAH!

WE GOTTA
GET OUTTA
HERE
NOW!

FOLLOW
ME, I HAVE
AN IDEA.

NO, NO, NO, NO, *NO!!!!!*

MR. WATERNOOSE!

JAMES! PERFECT TIMING. SHOW THESE MONSTERS HOW IT'S DONE.

SIR...I... BUT, SIR...

COME ON, COME ON! WHAT ARE YOU WAITING FOR? *ROAR!*

RAAAAAHRR

GENTLEMEN, I HOPE YOU LEARNED A VALUABLE LESSON IN SCARING TODAY.

BOO? BOO, IT'S ME, *KITTY.*

UMPH!

THUD

THE CHILD!

"ABOMINABLE!" CAN YOU BELIEVE THAT?!

WHY CAN'T THEY CALL ME, "THE *ADORABLE* SNOWMAN?"

SNOWCONE? OH, DON'T WORRY. IT'S LEMON.

LOOK AT THAT BIG JERK! BECAUSE OF HIM, I'M STUCK IN THIS FROZEN WASTELAND.

WASTELAND? I THINK YOU MEAN "WONDERLAND!" WAIT 'TIL YOU SEE THE LOCAL VILLAGE...

A *VILLAGE?* WHERE IS IT?

AT THE BOTTOM OF THE MOUNTAIN, AT LEAST A THREE-DAY HIKE!

THREE DAYS? AHHHHRR!

THUD

SWISSH

THE SLIDING ICE GIVES SULLEY AN IDEA...

YOU WANT TO GO TO THE VILLAGE?

WE NEED TO RESCUE BOO. NOTHING ELSE MATTERS.

NOTHING ELSE *MATTERS?* WHAT ABOUT *ME?* I'M YOUR *BEST FRIEND!*

BANG! BANG!

189

BOO'S IN TROUBLE. THERE MIGHT BE A WAY TO SAVE HER, IF WE CAN JUST GET DOWN TO THE VILLAGE...

IF YOU WANT TO GO, YOU'RE ON YOUR OWN.

DESPERATELY, SULLIVAN SPEEDS THROUGH THE DARKNESS... DODGING BOULDERS...

WOOOSH!

...WELL, NOT ALL OF THEM.

CRASH!

AAAUGH!

THUD

OOOF!

DAZED, SULLIVAN HEARS A CHILD'S SCREAM!

EEEEEEEE

MEANWHILE, BACK AT MONSTERS, INC....

~WHIMPER.~

AARGH!

SBRANG

KITTY!

BUT WILL SULLEY BE IN TIME TO SAVE BOO?

I NEVER SHOULD'VE BROUGHT YOU IN ON THIS, RANDALL.

BECAUSE OF YOU, I HAD TO BANISH MY TOP SCARER.

EH, SULLIVAN GOT WHAT HE DESERVED.

WHIIIIRRRRRRRRRRRRRRRRRRRRRRRRR

EEEEEEEE!

KITTY! KITTY! EEEEEEEEEH!

BOO?! NO! NOOOOOOOO!

RAAAHHHRRR

UGH!

CRASH!

KITTY!

I'M SORRY, BOO. LET'S GET OUT OF HERE!

191

STOP HIM! DON'T LET THEM GET AWAY!

OOF!

RANDALL KNOCKS SULLIVAN INTO THE HALLWAY!

THUD

OOOH!

SMACK

HUH?

IT'S NOT THAT I DON'T CARE ABOUT THE KID. I WAS MAD... I NEEDED SOME TIME TO THINK...BUT YOU SHOULDN'T HAVE LEFT ME OUT THERE!

I'M BEING ATTACKED!

OOF! UGH!

I'M NOT ATTACKING YOU! I'M BARING MY SOUL HERE. THE LEAST YOU COULD DO IS PAY ATTENTION!

PAF

UGH!

OOOF! OOOOOOOOOOH.

HEY, LOOK, IT'S RANDALL... OOOHH!

THUD

GET UP! THERE CAN'T BE ANY WITNESSES!

DON'T WORRY, THERE WON'T BE.

192

I'M GLAD YOU CAME BACK, MIKE!

HEY, **SOMEBODY** HAS TO TAKE CARE OF YOU, YOU BIG HAIRBALL!

SUDDENLY...

YAAAAAAAAH!

WHOA!

OOOF!

BONK

SHMOOPSIE POO! I REALLY CAN'T TALK...

MICHAEL, IF YOU DON'T TELL ME WHAT'S GOING ON **RIGHT NOW**, WE ARE **THROUGH**!

COME ON!

OK, HERE'S THE TRUTH! YOU KNOW THE KID THAT THEY'RE LOOKING FOR? SULLEY LET HER IN. WE TRIED TO SEND HER BACK, BUT WATERNOOSE HAS A SECRET PLOT AND NOW RANDALL'S RIGHT BEHIND US, AND HE'S TRYING TO KILL US!

YOU EXPECT ME TO BELIEVE THAT PACK OF LIES, MIKE WAZOWSKI?

MIKE WAZOWSKI!

GASP!

ATTENTION, EMPLOYEES! RANDALL BOGGS HAS JUST BROKEN THE ALL-TIME SCARE RECORD!

THERE THEY ARE!

NICE JOB!

WAY TO GO, RANDALL!

ALRIGHT, ALRIGHT! GET OUT OF MY WAY!

GO GET 'EM, GOOGLEY BEAR!

SUCCESS LOOKS CLOSE!

THERE IT IS!

BUT NOT CLOSE ENOUGH. BOO'S DOOR IS JUST OUT OF REACH AND RANDALL IS GAINING GROUND!

BUT SULLIVAN ISN'T GIVING UP! GRABBING ANOTHER DOOR, HE SAILS INTO THE VAULT.

GRAB ON MIKE!

ARE YOU OUT OF YOUR... AAAAAH!

DON'T LOOK DOWN!

WHEEEE!

BOO'S DOOR IS DEAD AHEAD WHEN...

...THE TRIO'S DOOR COMES TO A DEAD END! RANDALL STARTS CLOSING IN! THEY NEED POWER, AND FAST!

MIKE, MAKE BOO LAUGH!

OOF! OW!

GET IT OPEN!

WHY COULDN'T WE BE BANISHED HERE?

COME ON, WE GOTTA FIND ANOTHER DOOR!

SULLEY, JUMP! I'M RIGHT BEHIND YA!

I HOPE THAT HURT, LIZARD BOY!

SLAM

BUT THEY HAVEN'T LOST RANDALL YET! SUDDENLY...

GRRRRR!

EEEEEE!!!

NICE WORKIN' WITH YA!

AAAHH!

I'M TRYING!

GET IT OPEN!

WOOOOOSH

SMASH

WHEW!

THERE THEY ARE! GRAB ON!

LOOKS LIKE WE CAUGHT THE EXPRESS!

WOOOOOSH

SULLEY AND MIKE GAIN ON RANDALL...GETTING CLOSER AND CLOSER, UNTIL...

UNGH!

OOF!

IT LOOKS BAD FOR SULLEY...

YOU'VE BEEN NUMBER ONE FOR TOO LONG, SULLIVAN!

KITTY!

YAAAAAA!!!

SHE'S NOT SCARED OF YOU ANYMORE, RANDALL! YOU'RE OUT OF A JOB!

RAARRR!

AAAAAAAAHHHHH

HERE'S THE PITCH--

AND HE IS OUTTA HERE!

RANDALL GETS WHAT'S COMING TO HIM AT LAST!

MAMA, 'NOTHER 'GATOR GOT IN THE HOUSE.

GO GET THE SHOVEL.

THUMP CRUNCH

HOUP! UMPH! OWWWWW!

WINA ASA OHER!

EXCITEDLY, BOO POINTS OUT HER DOOR. THE BOYS GRAB HOLD, BUT SUDDENLY SOMETHING GOES WRONG.

WHAT'S HAPPENING?!

HOLD ON!

COME OUT WITH THE CHILD IN PLAIN SIGHT!

OK, YOU GOT US. BUT BEFORE YOU TAKE US AWAY, I HAVE ONE THING TO SAY.

NYAH-NYAH-NYAH!

STOP HIM!

AS THE CDA AGENTS TAKE OFF AFTER MIKE...

WHAT THE...HE HAS THE CHILD!

CRASH!

197

I JUST WANT TO SEND HER HOME.

VERY GOOD. SOMEONE BRING ME A DOOR SHREDDER.

YOU MEAN, I CAN'T SEE HER AGAIN?

THAT'S THE WAY IT HAS TO BE. I'LL GIVE YOU FIVE MINUTES.

NOTHING'S COMING OUT OF THE CLOSET TO SCARE YOU ANYMORE. RIGHT?

BABJAWADA.

KITTY.

GOODBYE, BOO. KITTY HAS TO LEAVE.

TLACK

BOO! KITTY?

NONE OF THIS EVER HAPPENED, GENTLEMEN. AND I DON'T WANT TO SEE ANY PAPERWORK ON THIS.

RRRRRRRRRRRRRRRR

THEY'RE TAKING MR. WATERNOOSE AWAY. THE FACTORY WILL SHUT DOWN!

THERE'LL BE EVEN LESS SCREAM TO GO AROUND! EEEEEE!

CHEER UP, PAL. WE GOT HER HOME. ALRIGHT, WE'RE BOTH OUT OF A JOB; BUT YOU KNOW, WE HAD SOME LAUGHS ALONG THE WAY.

SUDDENLY, SULLIVAN HAS A BRILLIANT IDEA!

IS THIS THING ON? HELLO? TESTING...HEY, HOW ARE YA? YOU'RE IN KINDERGARTEN, RIGHT...I LOVED KINDERGARTEN, BEST THREE YEARS OF MY LIFE.

AH...

OW!

THUMP

HA, HA, HA!

GREAT JOB, MIKEY! YOU FILLED YOUR QUOTA ON THE FIRST KID OF THE DAY! LAUGHTER IS TEN TIMES MORE POWERFUL THAN SCREAM!

NOT BAD, HUH?

HEY, DID YOU BRING THE MAGAZINE?

THEY JUST DELIVERED A WHOLE BOX!

WE MADE THE COVER, RIGHT?

THAT'S WHAT THEY SAID.

OH GOGGLEY-BEAR!

I'M ON THE COVER OF A MAGAZINE!

Business Shrie

MONSTERS, INC. BACK ON TOP!

THINGS HAVE NEVER BEEN BETTER AT MONSTERS, INC.

BUT SOMETHING'S MISSING FOR SULLIVAN...

HEY, SULL, I WANT TO SHOW YOU SOMETHING.

MIKE, IS THAT HER?

SORRY IT TOOK SO LONG PAL, THERE WAS A LOT OF WOOD TO GO THROUGH. IT ONLY WORKS IF EVERY PIECE IS IN PLACE.

BOO!

KITTY!

THE END

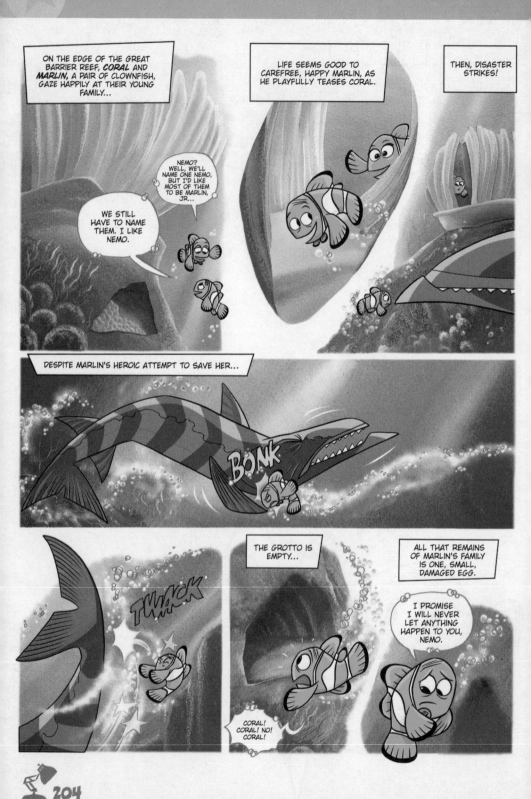

MEANWHILE, NEMO IS PLUNGED INTO A STRANGE, NEW PLACE...

GASP!

...AN AQUARIUM IN A DENTIST'S OFFICE.

FOUND THAT POOR LITTLE GUY ON THE REEF. SO, THAT NOVOCAINE KICKED IN YET?

BUUUBBLES! MY BUBBLES!

AAAAH!

SLOW DOWN, LITTLE FELLA.

AW, HE'S SCARED.

I WANNA GO HOME. DO YOU KNOW WHERE MY DAD IS?

YOUR DAD'S PROBABLY BACK AT THE PET STORE.

I'M FROM THE OCEAN.

AAAH! HE HASN'T BEEN DECONTAMI-NATED YET!

VOILA! HE IS CLEAN!

IF THERE'S ANYTHING YOU NEED JUST ASK YOUR AUNTIE DEB. IF I'M NOT AROUND YOU CAN ALWAYS ASK MY SISTER, FLO.

WE GOT A LIVE ONE! ROOT CANAL, AND IT'S NOT GOING TO BE PRETTY!

OH BOY!

YEAH, BABY!

LET'S CHECK IT OUT!

WHAT'D HE USE TO OPEN? A GATOR-GLIDDEN DRILL. NOW HE'S USING A HEDSTROEM FILE. NO, IT'S NOT.

ALRIGHT, YOU CAN GO AHEAD AND RINSE.

WHAT DID I MISS?

HEY, NIGEL. A ROOT CANAL, AND IT'S A DOOZY.

HELLO, WHO'S THIS?

NEW GUY. THE DENTIST TOOK HIM OFF THE REEF.

NO, NO, THOSE AREN'T YOUR FISH! GO ON! SHOO!

THUNK

THIS IS *DARLA*, MY NIECE. GONNA BE *EIGHT* THIS WEEK. YOU'RE HER PRESENT. SHE'S GONNA BE HERE FRIDAY TO PICK YOU UP.

OH, DARLA, NOT HER!

WHAT? WHAT'S WRONG WITH HER?

SHE'S A FISH KILLER.

POOR CHUCKLES. HE WAS HER PRESENT LAST YEAR. HITCHED A RIDE ON THE PORCELAIN EXPRESS.

SHE WOULDN'T STOP SHAKING THE BAG!

I CAN'T GO WITH THAT GIRL! I HAVE TO GET HOME. I HAVE TO GET BACK WITH MY DAD. HE DOESN'T KNOW WHERE I AM!

DADDY! HELP ME!

HE'S STUCK! WE GOTTA GET HIM OUTTA THERE! WHAT DO WE DO?

NOBODY TOUCH HIM.

YOU GOT YOURSELF IN THERE, YOU CAN GET YOURSELF OUT.

I-I CAN'T. I HAVE A BAD FIN.

NEVER STOPPED ME.

I CAN'T.

JUST THINK ABOUT WHAT YOU NEED TO DO.

PERFECT!

PRETTY GOOD KID!

YOU DID IT!

YAY!

UH, OH. I'VE SEEN THAT LOOK BEFORE.

I'M THINKIN'.

WHAT'S YOUR NAME, KID?

NEMO. I'M NEMO.

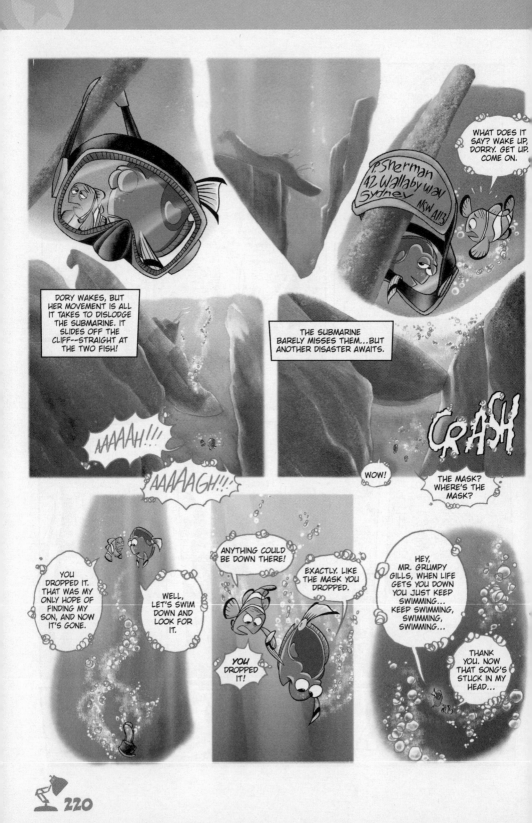

LATE THAT SAME NIGHT, IN THE DENTIST'S OFFICE A STRANGE CEREMONY TAKES PLACE...

YOU HAVE BEEN CALLED FORTH TO THE SUMMIT OF MOUNT WANNAHOCKALOOGIE TO JOIN WITH US IN THE FRATERNAL BONDS OF TANKHOOD...

...IF YOU ARE ABLE TO SWIM THROUGH THE RING OF FIRE!

FROM THIS MOMENT ON YOU WILL NOW BE KNOWN AS "SHARK BAIT."

OOOH, HA-HA!

OK, *SHARK BAIT'S* ONE OF *US* NOW. AND WE CAN'T SEND HIM OFF TO HIS DEATH. SO WE'RE GONNA HELP HIM ESCAPE. WE'RE *ALL* GONNA ESCAPE.

NOT ANOTHER ONE OF YOUR PLANS...

THEY *NEVER* WORK.

SEE THAT FILTER? YOU'RE THE ONLY ONE SMALL ENOUGH TO GET IN AND OUT OF THAT THING. YOU TAKE A PEBBLE IN THERE AND JAM THE GEARS. THIS TANK'S GONNA GET FILTHY.

THE DENTIST WILL HAVE TO CLEAN THE TANK, AND WHEN HE DOES, HE'LL TAKE US OUT OF THE TANK, PUT US IN PLASTIC BAGS...

...WE'LL THEN ROLL OURSELVES DOWN THE COUNTER... ...OUT THE WINDOW, OFF THE AWNING, INTO THE BUSHES...

...ACROSS THE STREET AND INTO THE HARBOR. WHAT DO YOU THINK?

LET'S DO IT!

MEANWHILE, IN THE AQUARIUM, GILL TEACHES NEMO TO SWIM BETTER...

YOU'RE LOOKIN' AT MY SCARS, AREN'T YOU? THIS ONE HAPPENED WHEN I LANDED ON DENTAL TOOLS. I WAS AIMING FOR THE TOILET.

THE TOILET?

ALL DRAINS LEAD TO THE OCEAN, KID.

YOU MISS YOUR DAD, DON'T YOU? YOU'RE LUCKY TO HAVE SOMEONE OUT THERE WHO'S LOOKIN' FOR YOU.

HE'S NOT LOOKING FOR ME. HE'S SCARED OF THE OCEAN.

HE'S LEAVING! YOUR CUE, NEMO!

THERE'S A GAP ABOVE THE BIG WATER WHEEL JUST BIG ENOUGH FOR YOU TO LEAP THROUGH. THEN, SWIM TO THE BOTTOM OF THE CHAMBER.

NICELY DONE. HERE COMES THE PEBBLE.

WEDGE THAT PEBBLE UP AGAINST THE ROD TO STOP IT TURNING.

GILL, THIS ISN'T A GOOD IDEA. HE'S JUST A KID.

NEMO SUCCEEDS! BUT AS HE SWIMS BACK UP THE TUBE, THE PEBBLE SLIPS OUT!

GILL!

GET HIM OUTTA THERE!

WHAT DO WE DO? WHAT DO WE DO?

COME ON, SHARKBAIT! GRAB THIS!

PULL!

GILL, DON'T MAKE HIM GO BACK IN THERE.

NO. WE'RE DONE.

HEY! LOOK, EVERYBODY! GO ON! JUMP ON HIM!

DID YOU REALLY CROSS THE JELLYFISH FOREST?

DID THEY STING YOU?

DID YOU DIE? WHERE YOU GOIN'?

WELL, MY SON, NEMO WAS TAKEN AWAY FROM ME...

GASP!

ALRIGHT, KIDS. I NEED TO BREATHE.

FATHER TELLS HIS STORY, AND IT BEGINS TO SPREAD THROUGHOUT THE OCEAN...

...GOLLY, THAT'S AMAZING...

...THEY BUMP INTO THREE FEROCIOUS SHARKS. HE SCARES THEM...

...AND THESE TWO LITTLE FISH HAVE BEEN SEARCHING THE OCEAN FOR DAYS--ON THE EAST AUSTRALIAN CURRENT-- WHICH MEANS THAT HE MAY BE ON...

...HIS WAY RIGHT NOW. THAT SHOULD PUT HIM IN SYDNEY HARBOR...

...IN A MATTER OF DAYS. THAT'S ONE DEDICATED FATHER, IF YOU ASK ME.

HAVE YOU EVER SEEN SUCH BEAUTIFUL FILTH? AND IT'S ALL THANKS TO YOU, LAD.

ME? WOW!

WHAT A STATE! I BETTER CLEAN THE FISH TANK BEFORE DARLA GETS HERE TOMORROW.

HE'S GONNA CLEAN THE TANK! WE DID IT!

AND YOUR DAD'S PROBABLY WAITING FOR YOU IN THE HARBOR.

MEANWHILE, IN THE BELLY OF THE WHALE...

WILL YOU STOP IT?! WE'RE IN A WHALE! DON'T YOU GET IT?

WHEEE! A WHALE? WOW! YOU KNOW, I SPEAK WHALE!

... I HAVE TO GET OUT. I HAVE TO FIND MY SON. I HAVE TO TELL HIM HOW OLD SEA TURTLES ARE. I PROMISED HIM I'D NEVER LET ANYTHING HAPPEN TO HIM.

THAT'S A FUNNY THING TO PROMISE. YOU CAN'T NEVER LET ANYTHING HAPPEN TO HIM. THEN NOTHING WOULD EVER HAPPEN TO HIM. NOT MUCH FUN FOR LITTLE HARPO.

BOOM BOOM BOOM

HMM. HE SAID WE SHOULD GO TO THE BACK OF THE THROAT...

OF COURSE HE WANTS US TO GO THERE! THAT'S EATING US!

BOOM BOOM

HE SAYS IT'S TIME TO LET GO! EVERYTHING'S GONNA BE ALRIGHT. JUST HAVE A LITTLE FAITH AND LET GO!

NEMO!

AAAAAH!!

233

WOOOSH

AAAAHHH!!!

LOOK! S-SI-SIDN— SYDNEY!

SYDNEY NEW SOUTH WALE

WE'RE GONNA FIND MY SON! ALL WE HAVE TO DO IS FIND THE BOAT THAT TOOK HIM.

WELL, THIS'LL BE EASY.

YOU WERE RIGHT, DORY. WE MADE IT!

BUT IN THE CITY, PLANS HAVE GONE AWRY AND TIME IS RUNNING OUT.

IT'S MORNING, EVERYONE! THE SUN IS SHINING, THE TANK IS CLEAN...AND *THE TANK IS CLEAN!*

THE BOSS MUST HAVE INSTALLED A NEW SYSTEM LAST NIGHT WHILE WE WERE SLEEPING.

THE AQUASCUM IS PROGRAMMED TO CLEAN YOUR TANK EVERY FIVE MINUTES.

CURSE YOU, AQUASCUM.

THE ESCAPE PLAN IS RUINED.

WHAT ARE WE GONNA DO?

DARLA!

STAY DOWN, KID!

THIS TIME IT'S A FALSE ALARM, BUT NEMO'S STILL NOT OUT OF DANGER...

SUDDENLY...

HELP ME. HELP, HELP, HELP!

HOLD ON, I'M COMIN'. SHARKBAIT.

C'MON KID, SWIM DOWN. SWIM DOWN!

JUMP IN AND SWIM DOWN!

THE TANK FISH SUCCEED IN PULLING THE NET DOWN, BUT NEMO GETS CAUGHT IN A PLASTIC BAG.

GILL!

NOW, WHERE'S THAT TRAY?

ROLL, KID! ROLL!

NOW THAT WOULD BE A NASTY FALL.

GILL, I DON'T WANT TO GO BELLY UP!

CALM DOWN, NEMO. YOU'RE GONNA BE OK!

RIIING

GASP!

235

HEY, I FOUND SUPERFISH!

WHERE'S NEMO?

LOOK AT THE DENTIST! QUICK!

NIGEL, GET IN THERE!

I CAN'T GO IN THERE!

OH, YES YOU CAN!

WHAT THE--

POP

SPLASH

NEMO PLAYS DEAD TO ESCAPE DARLA... BUT MARLIN DOESN'T UNDERSTAND. TIME SEEMS TO STOP FOR HIM...

MARLIN GIVES ONE LAST MUFFLED CRY AS HE AND DORY ARE TRAPPED INSIDE NIGEL'S BEAK...

NEMO HEARS HIS DAD'S VOICE...BUT TOO LATE.

GET OUT WITH YA!

NEMO

DADDY?

QUICK! TO THE TOP OF MOUNT WANNA-HOCKALOOGIE! WE HAVE TO SAVE NEMO!

FISHY, FISHY.

RING OF FIRE!

HURRY! NEMO CAN'T BREATHE!

AAAH!

SMACK

KRIKEY!

THUNK

GO, GILL, GO!

TELL YOUR DAD I SAID HI.

THUD

WHOA!

WHOA!

WHOA!

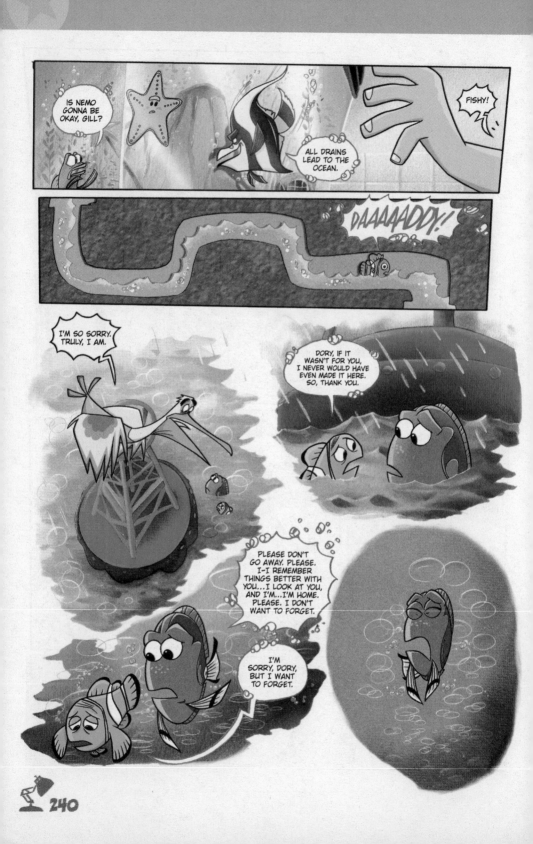

DORY DID NOT REMEMBER WHO NEMO WAS UNTIL SHE READ THE WORD, "SYDNEY" ON THE WATER PIPE LOGO.

HUH?! NEMO! IT'S YOU! YOU'RE NEMO! YOUR FATHER ISN'T GONNA... OH, YOUR FATHER....

YOU KNOW MY DAD?! WHERE IS HE?

HE WENT THIS WAY-- QUICK!

HEY, LOOK OUT!

I'M SORRY. JUST TRYING TO GET HOME.

HAVE YOU SEEN AN ORANGE FISH SWIM BY HERE?

YEAH, BUT I'M NOT TELLING YOU WHERE HE WENT!

MINE! MINE!

OK, I'LL TALK! I'LL TALK! HE WENT TO THE FISHING GROUNDS.

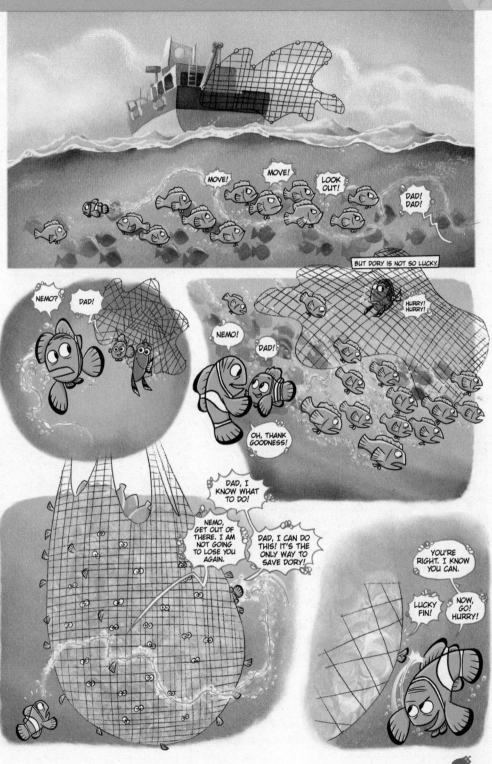

245

THE INCREDIBLES

253

I'M *INCREDIBOY!*

BUDDY? LOOK, I'VE BEEN NICE. I'VE STOOD FOR EVERY PHOTO, SIGNED EVERY SCRAP OF PAPER, BUT THIS - THIS IS A BIT MUCH.

MY NAME IS *INCREDIBOY!* I KNOW ALL YOUR MOVES, CRIME FIGHTING STYLE, CATCH PHRASES- EVERYTHING! I'M YOUR NUMBER ONE FAN!

SHPOOOMPH

MR. INCREDIBLE IS ALREADY ON TO HIS NEXT CRIME STOP...

YOU KNOW, YOU CAN TELL A LOT ABOUT A WOMAN BY THE CONTENTS OF HER PURSE. BUT MAYBE THAT'S NOT WHAT YOU HAD IN MIND...

?

SOCK

ELASTIGIRL. IT'S ALL RIGHT, I'VE GOT HIM.

THANKS, BUT I DON'T NEED ANY HELP.

WHAT EVER HAPPENED TO "LADIES FIRST?"

WHAT EVER HAPPENED TO "EQUAL TREATMENT?"

SOCK

HEY... THE LADY GOT ME FIRST.

SURE, YOU'VE GOT HIM. A SIMPLE "THANK YOU" WILL SUFFICE.

I WORK ALONE.

YOU NEED TO BE MORE...

...FLEXIBLE.

YOU DOING ANYTHING LATER?

I HAVE A PREVIOUS ENGAGEMENT.

FHWEEEW.

HEY, FROZONE!

SHOULDN'T YOU BE GETTING READY?

HEY, I'VE STILL GOT TIME.

HE'S GOING TO JUMP!

OOF!

CRASH

MY COLLAR BONE - I THINK YOU BROKE IT.

WITH COUNSELING, I THINK YOU WILL COME TO FORGIVE ME -

WAIT A MINUTE...

SHOWTIME --!

FLIP! FLAP! CHSSSS CHUNGK

ROBERT GOLDEN, DO YOU TAKE THIS WOMAN TO BE YOUR LAWFUL WEDDED WIFE...

CUTTING IT KIND OF CLOSE, DON'T CHA THINK?

YOU'VE GOT TO BE MORE... "FLEXIBLE."

I LOVE YOU, BUT IF WE'RE GOING TO MAKE THIS WORK, YOU'VE GOT TO BE MORE THAN MR. INCREDIBLE, YOU KNOW THAT, DON'T YOU?

... AS LONG AS YOU BOTH SHALL LIVE?

I DO.

AS LONG AS WE BOTH SHALL LIVE. NO MATTER WHAT HAPPENS.

WE'RE SUPERS. WHAT COULD HAPPEN?

FIVE DAYS LATER, ANOTHER SUIT WAS FILED BY THE VICTIMS IN THE EL-TRAIN ACCIDENT...

INCREDIBLE'S COURT LOSSES COST THE GOVERNMENT MILLIONS, AND OPENED THE FLOOD GATES FOR LAWSUITS THE WORLD OVER...

...THE GOVERNMENT CREATED THE SUPER PROTECTION PROGRAM, NO LONGER HOLDING SUPERS ACCOUNTABLE FOR THE PAST IF THEY BECOME AVERAGE CITIZENS AND NEVER RESUME HERO WORK.

DAILY NEWS
MR. INCREDIBLE SUED-
EXTRA
MR. INCREDIBLE

259

STOP IT! DASH! VIOLET!

BEE-YABA!

BOB?? IT'S TIME TO ENGAGE!! I NEED YOU TO INTERVENE!

WHAM!

ooF!

SIMON J. PALADINO, LONG AN OUTSPOKEN ADVOCATE OF SUPERHERO RIGHTS, IS MISSING.

GAZERBEAM?

BUH-DAAA!

OKAY – I'M INTERVENING, I'M INTERVENING!

DING-DONG

HOIST!

HEY LUCIUS!

HEY SPEEDO... HEY HELEN

I'LL BE BACK LATER.

OH, RIGHT. BOWLING NIGHT. SAY HELLO TO HONEY FOR ME, LUCIUS.

...SO NOW, WITH ONE MORE JOLT OF THE DEATH RAY I'M AN EPITAPH, AND WHAT DOES BARON VON RUTHLESS DO? HE STARTS MONOLOGUING! ABOUT HOW FEEBLE I AM HOW THE WHOLE WORLD WILL BE HIS --

FIRE AT FOURTH AND ELIAS.

A FIRE! WE'RE CLOSE! LET'S GO!

THAT WAS TOO CLOSE. WE ARE NOT DOING THAT AGAIN.

TRUST ME. THIS IS THE ONE HE'S BEEN LOOKING FOR...

I THOUGHT YOU'D BE BACK BY ELEVEN. IS THIS.. RUBBLE?

WELL... THE BUILDING WAS COMING DOWN ANYWAY.

WHAT-? YOU KNOCKED DOWN A BUILDING?

IT WAS ON FIRE! STRUCTURALLY UNSOUND! IT WAS COMING DOWN ANYWAY! I PERFORMED A PUBLIC SERVICE. YOU ACT LIKE THAT'S A BAD THING!

IT IS A BAD THING, BOB! YOU CAN'T UPROOT OUR FAMILY AGAIN SO YOU CAN TO RELIVE THE GLORY DAYS!

IT'S BETTER THAN ACTING LIKE THEY DIDN'T HAPPEN!

OUR FAMILY IS WHAT'S HAPPENING NOW. YOU, ME, VI AND DASH!

YOU WANNA HELP DASH? LET HIM GO OUT FOR SPORTS!

YOU KNOW WHY WE CAN'T DO THAT!

BECAUSE HE'D BE GREAT!

?

FIIISSSH!

IT'S OKAY, KIDS. WE'RE JUST HAVING A DISCUSSION.

WE'RE SORRY WE WOKE YOU. EVERYTHING'S OKAY. GO BACK TO BED. IT'S LATE. IN FACT - WE SHOULD ALL BE IN BED.

MR. HUPH WANTS YOU IN HIS OFFICE.

NOW!

I'M NOT HAPPY, BOB. I CAN'T HANDLE YOUR CUSTOMERS' INEXPLICABLE KNOWLEDGE OF INSURICARE'S INNER WORKINGS.

WE'RE SUPPOSED TO HELP *OUR* PEOPLE, BOB, STARTING WITH OUR STOCKHOLDERS!

THAT MAN OUT THERE – HE'S GETTING MUGGED!

WELL, LET'S HOPE WE DON'T COVER HIM. STAY HERE, OR YOU'RE FIRED!

HE GOT AWAY...

GOOD THING, TOO. YOU WERE THIS CLOSE TO LOSING YOUR J –

WHAM

SQUEAK!

UH-OH.

MOAN.

HOURS LATER...

BOB, EVERY TIME YOU SAY "SOME ONE WAS IN TROUBLE AND I HAD TO DO SOMETHING," IT MEANS THOUSANDS OF TAXPAYER DOLLARS TO PAY DAMAGES AND RELOCATE YOUR FAMILY AGAIN.

NO, RICK. I CAN'T DO THAT TO MY FAMILY AGAIN. WE JUST GOT SETTLED. IT'LL BE ALL RIGHT. I'LL MAKE IT WORK. THANKS.

RIFFLE RIFFLE KLUNK!!

HUH?

MATCH: MR. INCREDIBLE.

WHA --?

ROOM IS SECURE. COMMENCE MESSAGE.

HELLO, MR. INCREDIBLE. MY NAME IS MIRAGE. I REPRESENT A TOP SECRET DIVISION OF THE GOVERNMENT. AN EXPERIMENTAL ROBOT HAS ESCAPED FROM OUR CONTROL.

HONEY?? DINNER'S READY! IS SOMEONE IN THERE?

NO, IT'S THE *TV!* I'M TRYING TO WATCH!

IF YOU ACCEPT THIS MISSION, YOUR PAYMENT WILL BE TRIPLE YOUR CURRENT ANNUAL SALARY.

YOU HAVE 24 HOURS TO CALL THE NUMBER ON THE CARD.

THIS MESSAGE WILL SELF-DESTRUCT.

BOOM!

SHWISSSSS!

TWISSSSSS!

YOU'RE ONE DISTRACTED GUY.

HMN...? I DON'T MEAN TO BE.

I KNOW YOU MISS BEING A HERO... AND YOUR JOB IS FRUSTRATING AND... AND I JUST WANT YOU TO KNOW HOW MUCH IT MEANS TO ME THAT YOU STAY AT IT ANYWAY.

HONEY, ABOUT THE JOB. UH, THE COMPANY'S SENDING ME TO A CONFERENCE OUT OF TOWN. I'LL BE GONE FOR A FEW DAYS.

THEY'VE NEVER SENT YOU TO A CONFERENCE BEFORE. MAYBE THEY'RE FINALLY RECOGNIZING YOUR TALENTS. IT'S WONDERFUL.

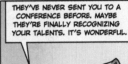

YES. YES, IT IS...

THIS IS MR. INCREDIBLE. I'M IN.

SOON BOB IS BACK, NOT AT A "BUSINESS CONFERENCE," BUT AT THE ISLAND OF NOMANISAN...

YOU WILL BE BRIEFED ON YOUR NEXT ASSIGNMENT IN THE CONFERENCE ROOM AT TWO O'CLOCK.

SWHISH!

GOT IT.

?

UHH!

FOOOOM!

PWAP!

R-R-R-R-R-RR!

IT'S BIGGER!

IT'S BADDER!

LADIES AND GENTLEMEN, IT'S TOO MUCH FOR MR. INCREDIBLE! WHOA-HO, HO!

WHIP WHIP

WHISHPWHIP

IT'S FINALLY READY! I WENT THROUGH QUITE A FEW SUPERS TO GET IT WORTHY TO FIGHT YOU, BUT MAN... IT WASN'T GOOD ENOUGH!

AFTER YOU TRASHED THE LAST ONE, I HAD TO MAKE SOME MODIFICATIONS. IT WAS DIFFICULT, BUT YOU ARE WORTH IT. AFTER ALL...

...I AM YOUR BIGGEST FAN.

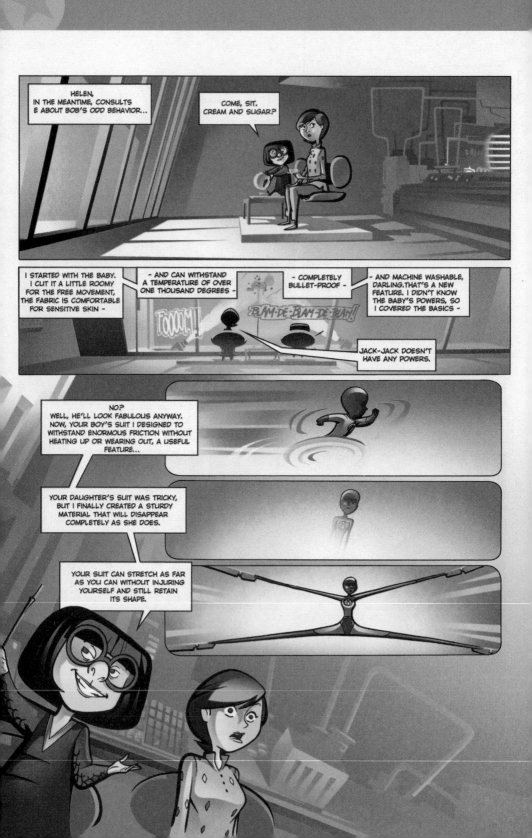

VIRTUALLY INDESTRUCTIBLE, YET IT BREATHES LIKE EGYPTIAN COTTON. WELL, DARLING, WHAT DO YOU THINK?

OUR FAMILY IS UNDERGROUND! BOB IS RETIRED! YOU HELPED HIM RESUME HERO WORK BEHIND MY BACK?

I ASSUMED YOU KNEW, DARLING! WHY WOULD HE KEEP SECRETS FROM YOU?

HE WOULDN'T! HE DIDN'T - DOESN'T!

SYNDROME'S OMNIDROID TESTS HAVE SO FAR ELIMINATED A WHO'S WHO OF SUPERS...

WHEW.

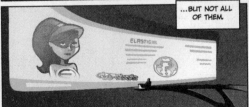

...BUT NOT ALL OF THEM.

274

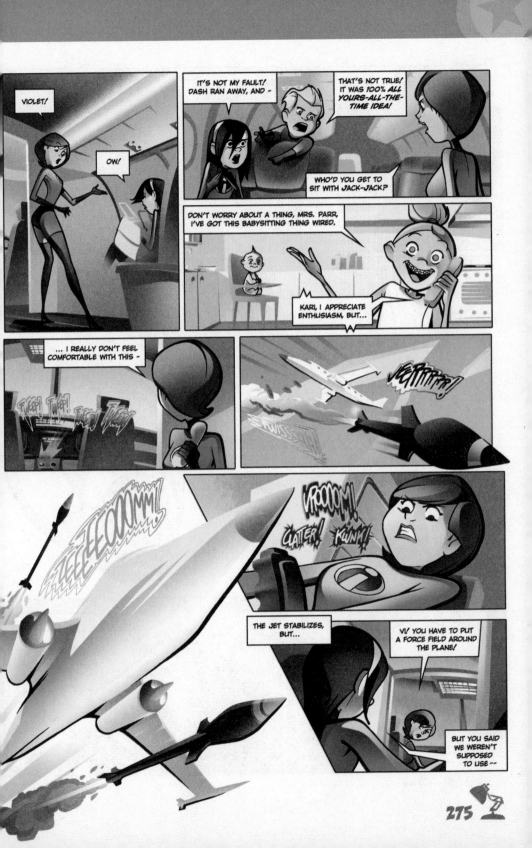

I KNOW WHAT I SAID. LISTEN TO WHAT I AM SAYING NOW.

I'VE NEVER DONE ONE THAT BIG BEFORE!

VIOLET!!! DO IT NOW!!

NO! CALL OFF THE MISSILES!! I'LL DO ANYTHING!!

TOO LATE. FIFTEEN YEARS TOO LATE.

SHOOF!

KA-BLOOOOOM

SWOOIP!

TARGET WAS DESTROYED.

AH, YOU'LL GET OVER IT. I SEEM TO RECALL YOU PREFER TO..."WORK ALONE."

SNAP! SNAP!

YARRGGH!

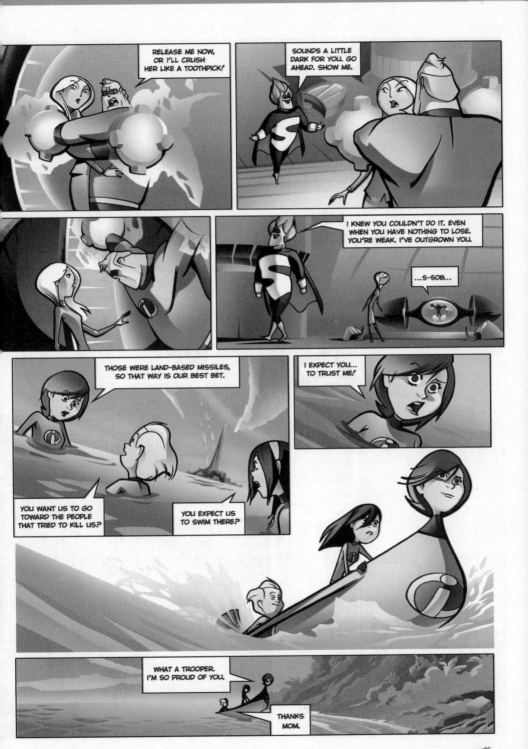

I'M GOING TO LOOK FOR YOUR FATHER. PUT THESE ON. YOUR IDENTITY IS YOUR MOST IMPORTANT POSSESSION. IF ANYTHING GOES WRONG, USE YOUR POWERS.

MOM, WHAT HAPPENED ON THE PLANE, I WANTED TO, I MEAN — I'M SO SORRY.

IT WASN'T FAIR FOR ME TO SUDDENLY ASK SO MUCH OF YOU BUT THINGS ARE DIFFERENT NOW. IF THE TIME COMES, YOU'LL KNOW WHAT TO DO. IT'S IN YOUR BLOOD.

HE'S NOT WEAK, YOU KNOW. VALUING LIFE IS NOT WEAKNESS.

HEY, I CALLED HIS BLUFF.

I KNEW HE WOULDN'T —

— AND DISREGARDING LIFE IS NOT STRENGTH. NEXT TIME YOU GAMBLE, BET YOUR OWN LIFE.

I'M NOT GONNA LEAVE THE CAVE. SHEESH!

I'M GONNA GO LOOK AROUND.

MOM SAID TO STAY HIDDEN.

THE DROID ROCKET IS BEING READIED FOR LIFTOFF...

... WHILE DEEP IN ITS EXHAUST TUNNEL, AN UNSUSPECTING DASH EXPLORES.

RRRRRRRRMMMBLE...

COOL!

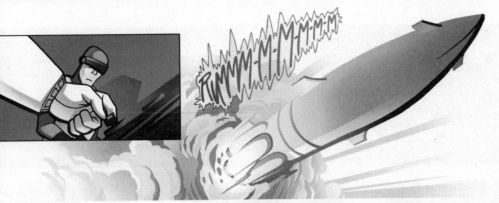

AIIEEYAAAAAHH!

VI! VI! VI!

WHAT DID YOU DO?

KA-BLAMMM!

THINGS QUIET DOWN FOR VI AND DASH UNTIL THE NEXT MORNING, WHEN THEIR COVER IS BLOWN...

ZWOOOOSH!

IDENTIFICATION, PLEASE! BWOOOZ! BWEEE! BWEEE! BWEEE!

WHAT DO WE DO? WHERE ARE WE GOING?

AWAY FROM HERE!! RUN!

THERE ISN'T MUCH TIME —

NO, THERE ISN'T. IN FACT —

— THERE'S NO TIME AT ALL. WHY ARE YOU HERE? WHAT MORE CAN YOU TAKE AWAY FROM ME?

FAMILY... SURVIVED THE CRASH ... THEY'RE HERE... ON THE ISLAND...

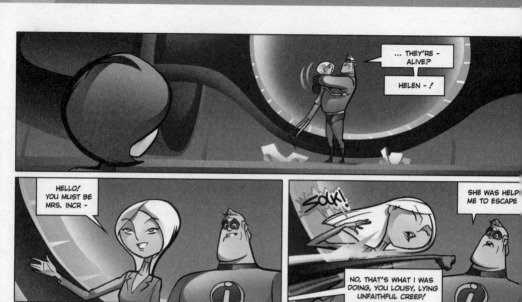

... THEY'RE - ALIVE?

HELEN - !

HELLO! YOU MUST BE MRS. INCR -

SOK!

SHE WAS HELP ME TO ESCAPE!

NO, THAT'S WHAT I WAS DOING, YOU LOUSY, LYING UNFAITHFUL CREEP!

HOW COULD I BETRAY THE PERFECT WOMAN?

OH, YOU'RE REFERRING TO ME NOW...

YOUR KIDS MIGHT'VE TRIGGERED THE ALERT. SECURITY'S BEEN SENT INTO THE JUNGLE.

DASH!! RUN!!

THEY'RE *SUPERS!* GET THE BOY!

REMEMBER WHAT MOM SAID.

WHAT?

HEY! STOP TALKING!

MOM! DAD!

FLOOMP!

KIDS! YOU'RE ALL RIGHT!

WE WERE SO WORRIED ABOUT YOU!

NYERRP!

VEEERR!

THWACK!

SOCK!

FOOOSSST!

BOOOM!

OH, I LOVE YOU!

285

THIS IS MY FAULT. I'VE BEEN SO OBSESSED WITH BEING UNDER-VALUED THAT I UNDER-VALUED ALL OF YOU. YOU ARE MY GREATEST ADVENTURE.

WELL, I THINK DAD HAS MADE EXCELLENT PROGRESS TODAY, BUT IT'S TIME TO WIND DOWN NOW...

OUR HEROES FIND THEIR WAY BACK TO THE HANGER...

A ROCKET'S FASTER THAN A JET.

I CAN'T FLY A ROCKET.

YOU DON'T HAVE TO. USE THE COORDINATES FROM THE LAST LAUNCH.

I'LL BET SYNDROME'S CHANGED THE PASSWORD BY NOW. HOW DO I GET INTO THE COMPUTER?

SAY PLEASE.

IN MUNICIBERG, A NEW "HERO" APPEARS...

STAND BACK! SOMEONE NEEDS TO TEACH THIS HUNK OF METAL A FEW MANNERS!

AAUUAGH!

R-R-R-RUMBLE!

C-C-CRACK

SMAAAGH!!

IT'S COMING BACK!

THE ONLY THING HARD ENOUGH TO PENETRATE IT IS...

...ITSELF!

IT DOESN'T WORK!

FooOOSH!

OOOP!

BA-BAA   BOOOM!

JUST LIKE OLD TIMES!

YEAH, JUST LIKE OLD TIMES, HA HA!

HURT THEN, TOO.

WE'VE FROZEN ALL SYNDROME'S ASSETS. IF HE EVEN SNEEZES WE'LL BE THERE WITH A HANKY AND HANDCUFFS. YOU DID GOOD.

HI, THIS IS KARI. THERE'S SOMETHING... UNUSUAL ABOUT JACK-JACK, AND I WAS GETTING REALLY WEIRDED OUT! BUT THANKS FOR SENDING THE REPLACEMENT SITTER...

BOB, LISTEN TO THIS...

THEY ARRIVE AT THE PARR HOUSE TO FIND...

AND IN TIME, WHO KNOWS? HE MIGHT MAKE A GOOD SIDEKICK...

CRAACK!

WAAAAAA...

YOU STOLE MY FUTURE. I'M RETURNING THE FAVOR. BUT DON'T WORRY. I'LL BE SUPPORTIVE, ENCOURAGING – EVERYTHING YOU WEREN'T.

WWAAAAAAAA...

...YYYAAAAEEE...

EEAAAGHHH!

295

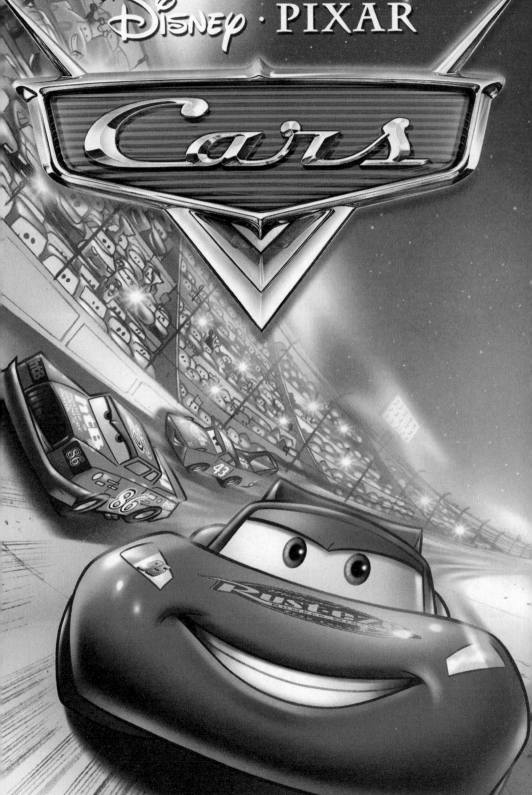

OKAY, HERE WE GO! I AM SPEED!

ONE WINNER! FORTY-TWO LOSERS!

I EAT LOSERS FOR BREAKFAST! MAYBE I SHOULD HAVE HAD BREAKFAST...

NO! STAY FOCUSED! I'M FASTER THAN FAST! QUICKER THAN QUICK! I AM...

HEY, LIGHTNING, YOU READY?

OH, YEAH! LIGHTNING'S READY! KA -CHOW!

MCQUEEN!

MCQUEEN!

WELCOME BACK TO THE DINOCO 400! I'M BOB CUTLASS HERE WITH DARRELL CARTRIP! THREE CARS ARE TIED FOR THE SEASON POINTS LEAD AND THE WINNER OF THIS FINAL RACE WILL WIN THE TITLE AND THE PISTON CUP!

MY OIL PRESSURE'S THROUGH THE ROOF!

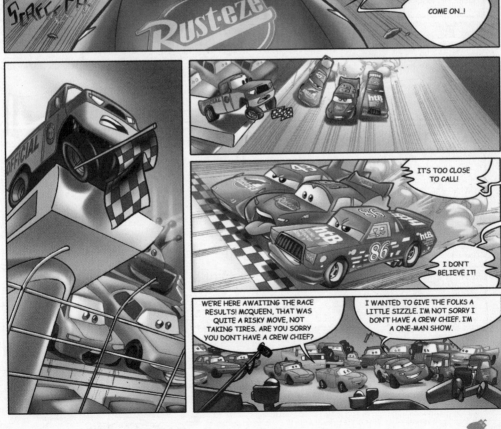

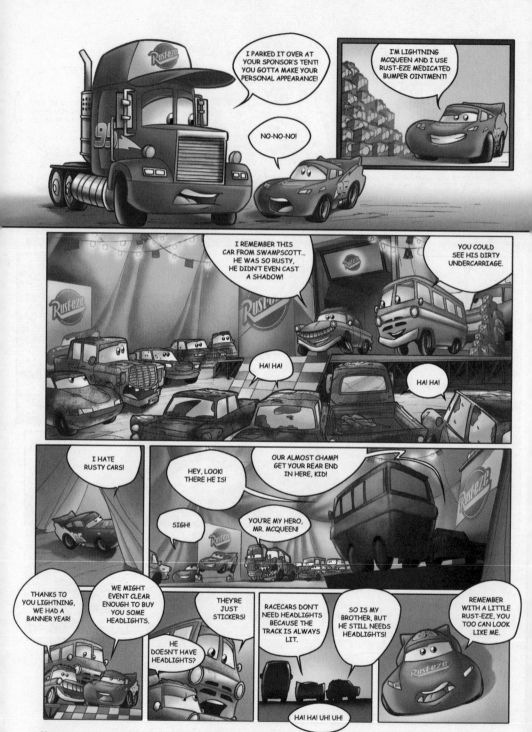

ALL NIGHT?

I NEED TO GET THERE BEFORE CHICK... AND HANG WITH DINOCO!

I'LL STAY UP WITH YOU!

ALL NIGHT?

"SURE! ALL NIGHT LONG!"

ZZZZZ

HEY YO DJ! WE GOT OURSELVES A NODDER!

A TOY IN THE TRAILER HITS A BUTTON AND MACK'S BACK DOOR OPENS...

LANE CHANGE, MAN!

95

BUMP

CLICK

95

ZZZZ

AHCHOOO!

GEZUNTHEIDT!

BANG

WHOA!

MACK

SCREECH

CR-R-RUNCH

THUD

SPROOING

BOY, YOU'RE IN A HEAP OF TROUBLE!

MORNING... ON THE WEST COAST...

WE'RE LIVE AT THE LOS ANGELES INTERNATIONAL SPEEDWAY, AS THE FIRST COMPETITOR, LIGHTNING MCQUEEN, IS ARRIVING AT THE TRACK!

WHAT DID MCQUEEN EAT FOR BREAKFAST?

IS MCQUEEN PREDICTING A VICTORY?

FLASH

OOOH!

FLASH

MCQUEEN'S DRIVER ARRIVED IN CALIFORNIA, BUT MCQUEEN WAS MISSING!

OH, BOY... WHAT...?

MORNING SLEEPIN' BEAUTY!

WHY DO I HAVE A PARKING BOOT ON?

YOU'RE FUNNY! MY NAME'S MATER, LIKE TUH-MATER, BUT WITHOUT THE "TUH"!

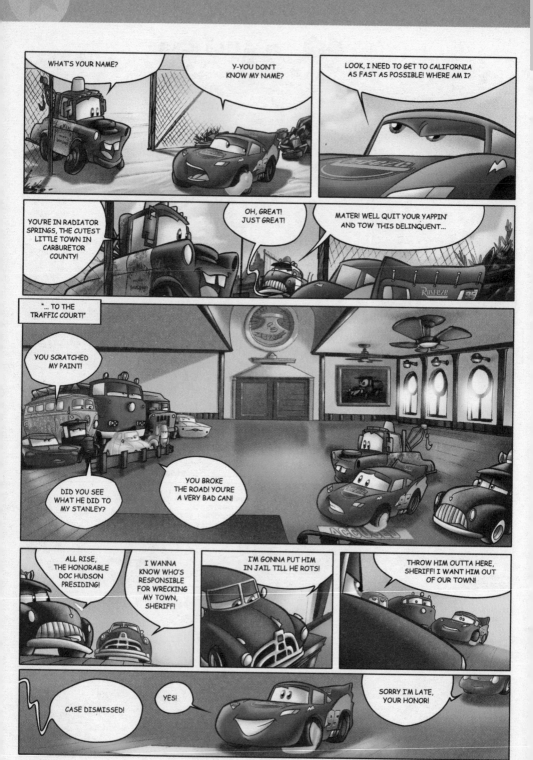

HOLY PORSCHE! SHE'S GOTTA BE FROM MY ATTORNEY'S OFFICE!

THANKS FOR COMING, BUT WE'RE ALL SET! HE'S LETTING ME GO!

HE'S LETTING YOU GO?

ME. YOU. DINNER?

UH... I'M GONNA TALK TO THE JUDGE.

HEY THERE, MATER!

HOWDY, SALLY!

YOU KNOW HER?

SHE'S THE TOWN ATTORNEY!

WHAT?

MAKE THIS GUY FIX THE ROAD, DOC! THE TOWN NEEDS THIS!

NO. I KNOW HIS TYPE. RACE CAR. HE'S THE LAST THING THIS TOWN NEEDS.

OKAY. I DIDN'T WANT TO HAVE TO DO THIS, BUT... FELLOW CITIZENS!

HERE SHE GOES AGAIN...

IT IS OUR JOB AND PLEASURE TO TAKE CARE OF THE TRAVELERS ON OUR STRETCH OF HIGHWAY 66, THE MOTHER ROAD!

WHAT TRAVELERS?

BUT HOW ARE WE TO CARE FOR THOSE TRAVELERS IF THERE IS NO ROAD FOR THEM TO DRIVE ON?

I WON'T SELL ANY TIRES!

I'LL GO OUT OF BUSINESS! WE'LL HAVE TO LEAVE TOWN!

SO WHAT DO YOU WANT THE CAR RESPONSIBLE TO DO?

FIX THE ROAD!

ORDER IN THE COURT!

OH, I AM SO NOT TAKING YOU TO DINNER!

THAT'S OKAY, STICKERS! YOU CAN TAKE BESSIE!

THIS HERE IS BESSIE, FINEST ROAD-PAVIN' MACHINE EVER BUILT!

WHAT? THIS PLACE IS CRAZY...

HOOK HIM UP, MATER!

OKEY DOKEY!

CLINK

FREEDOM!

MAYBE I SHOULD OF, UH, HOOKED 'IM UP TO BESSIE AND THEN TOOK THE BOOT OFF...

ZOOOM

VROOOM

GOODBYE RADIATOR SPRINGS! CALIFORNIA, HERE I COME!

SPUTT SPUTT

NO! OUTTA GAS! HOW CAN I BE OUT OF GAS?

BOY, WE AIN'T AS DUMB AS YOU THINK WE ARE!

WE SIPHONED YOUR GAS WHILE YOU WERE PASSED OUT!

GUIDO! WHY THE TIRES ARE HERE?

SONO SEMPRE STATI QUI! STAI SEMPRE A PARLARE...

I SHOULDN'T HAVE TO PUT UP WITH THIS! I'M A PRECISION INSTRUMENT OF SPEED AND AERODYNAMICS!

YOU HURT YOUR WHAT?

I'M A VERY FAMOUS RACE CAR!

A REAL RACE CAR? I HAVE FOLLOWED THE RACING MY ENTIRE LIFE!

THEN YOU KNOW WHO I AM! I'M LIGHTNING MCQUEEN!

DO YOU KNOW MANY FERRARIS?

NO, THEY RACE ON THE EUROPEAN CIRCUIT! I...

LUIGI FOLLOW ONLY THE FERRARIS!

I JUST DON'T SEE ANY ON-RAMP ANYWHERE!

IS THAT WHAT I THINK IT IS?

CUSTOMERS! ALRIGHT, NOBODY PANICS!

CUSTOMERS!

CUSTOMERS!

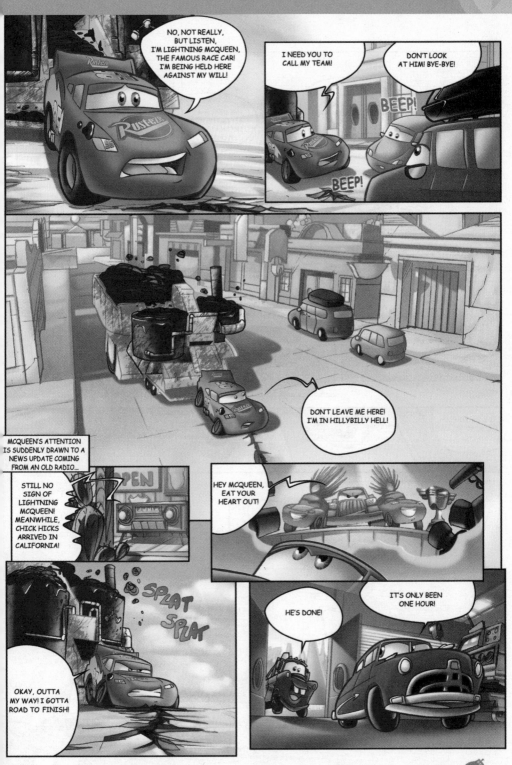

I'M THE F-F-FIRST O-ONE ON THE NEW ROAD! PRE-ETTY SMOO-OOTH!

I'M FINISHED! JUST SAY THANK YOU AND I'LL BE ON MY WAY!

IT LOOKS AWFUL.

THE DEAL WAS YOU FIX THE ROAD, NOT MAKE IT WORSE!

NOW SCRAPE IT OFF, START OVER AGAIN!

I'M NOT A BULLDOZER, I'M A RACE CAR!

IS THAT RIGHT? THEN WHY DON'T WE HAVE A LITTLE RACE?

ME AND YOU! IF YOU WIN, YOU GO AND I FIX THE ROAD!

WHAT?

IS THAT A JOKE?

I WIN, YOU DO THE ROAD MY WAY!

GENTLEMEN! START YOUR ENGINES!

PIT STOP?

I DON'T NEED ANY HELP. I WORK ALONE.

GREAT IDEA, DOC. NOW THE ROAD WILL NEVER GET DONE...

LUIGI?

UNO FOR THE MONEY, DUE FOR THE SHOW, TRE TO GET READY AND QUATTRO TO...

... GO!

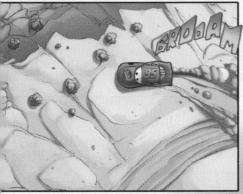

HUH? DOC, THE FLAG MEANS "GO"...

COME ON, MATER. MIGHT NEED A LITTLE HELP.

VARROOM

YOU GOT YOUR TOW CABLE!

I ALWAYS GOT MY TOW CABLE! WHY?

OH, JUST IN CASE!

BROOOM

AAAAAH!

YOU DRIVE LIKE YOU FIX ROADS! LOUSY!

OUCH!

I'M STARTIN' TO THINK HE KNOWED YOU WAS GONNA CRASH!

GRUNT! THANK YOU, MATER!

CRAZY GRANDPA CAR! TURN RIGHT...

... TO GO LEFT? HMMMM...

NO! GASP!

LATER...

OH, GUIDO! CHE BELLISSIMO! IT'S LOOK GREAT!

MATER, I NEED YOU TO WATCH THE PRISONER TONIGHT!

YES SIR!

SPLASH

WHOO! STOP! THAT'S COLD!

THANKS, RED!

WHAT WAS THAT FOR?

DO YOU WANT TO STAY AT THE COZY CONE? IF YOU DO YOU GOTTA BE CLEAN!

WAIT, YOU'RE BEING NICE TO ME?

HERE IT IS

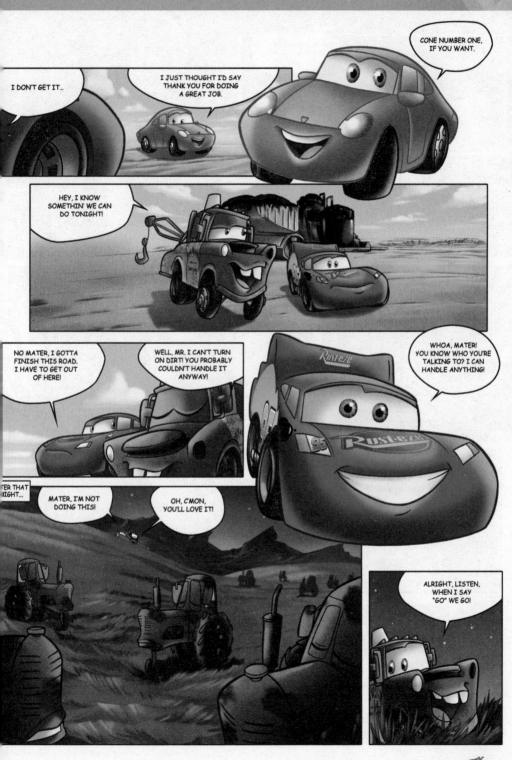

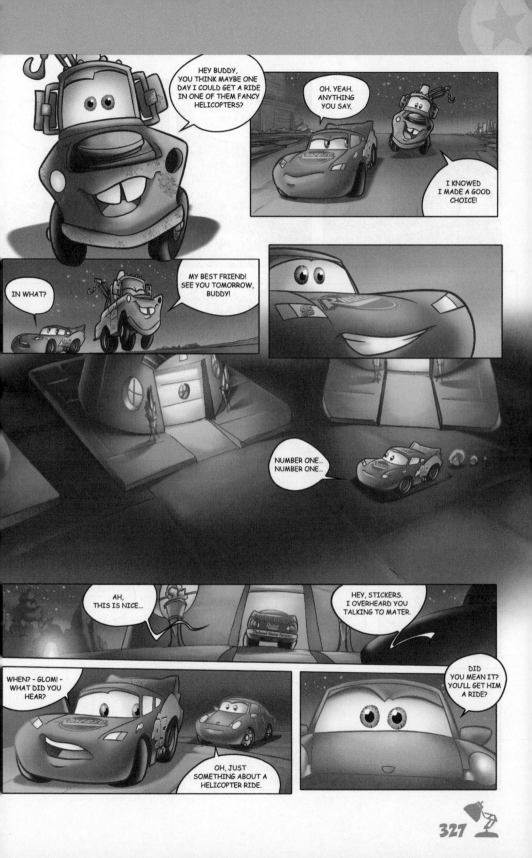

OH, WHO KNOWS? I GOTTA GET OUTTA HERE FIRST.

YOU KNOW, MATER TRUSTS YOU.

LOOK, I'M EXHAUSTED... IT'S KINDA BEEN A LONG DAY.

OKAY. GOOD NIGHT.

THE NEXT MORNING...

HAVE YOU SEEN THE SHERIFF? I...

...HEM! I-I JUST NEED MY DAILY GAS RATION!

WAIT FOR HIM AT FLO'S! NOW GET OUT OF HERE!

I'VE BEEN TRYNG TO GET OUT OF HERE FOR THREE DAYS...

STAY OUT

NO TRESPASS

NO KEEP OUT

KEEP OUT

HMMM... TIME TO CLEAN UP THE GARAGE DOC.

OH MY GOSH! THREE PISTON CUPS?

CHAMPION FOR ALL TIME!

THE SIGNS SAYS "STAY OUT"!

DOC! YOU HAVE THREE PISTON CUPS! HOW COULD YOU HAVE...

...YOU'RE "THE FABULOUS HUDSON HORNET"!

WAIT OVER AT FLO'S LIKE I TOLD YOU!

YOU GOTTA SHOW ME YOUR TRICKS, PLEASE!

I ALREADY TRIED THAT!

I MEAN, YOU WON THE CHAMPIONSHIP THREE TIMES! LOOK AT THOSE TROPHIES!

WHAT IS THIS PLACE?

HOW DOES A PORSCHE WIND UP IN A PLACE LIKE THIS?

SO I LEFT CALIFORNIA. JUST DROVE AND DROVE AND FINALLY BROKE DOWN RIGHT HERE.

DOC FIXED ME UP, FLO TOOK ME IN AND I NEVER LEFT.

WHEEL WELL. ...ED TO BE THE ...ST POPULAR ...TOP ON THE ...OTHER ROAD.

I WAS AN ATTORNEY IN L.A. THAT WAS MY LIFE... AND IT NEVER FELT HAPPY...

WHY DIDN'T YOU GO BACK?

I FELL IN LOVE...

... WITH THIS!

THE DAY OF THE BIG RACE!

HELLO RACE FANS AND WELCOME TO THE RACE OF THE CENTURY!

THERE'S A CROWD OF NEARLY TWO HUNDRED THOUSAND CARS HERE AT THE LOS ANGELES INTERNATIONAL SPEEDWAY!

HEY KING, GOOD LUCK ON YOUR LAST RACE.

THANKS. I APPRECIATE IT.

C'MON CHICK, LET'S SEE THE CLOUD!

SHOW US THE THUNDERCLOUD!

OKAY, HERE WE GO! I'M SPEED! I'M....

HEY LIGHTNING, YOU READY?

YOU WANNA KNOW THE FORECAST? 100% CHANCE OF THUNDER! KA-CHICK-A!

YEAH! I'M READY!

FLASH

FLASH

THANKS FOR BEING MY PIT CREW TODAY.

GO!

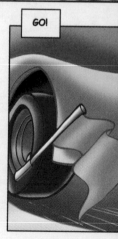

...SALLY...

WHERE YA BEEN, MCQUEEN? I'VE BEEN KIND OF LONELY EXCEPT FOR THE DINOCO FOLKS! KA CHICK-A!

WHOO-HOO! I WON, BABY!

WHAT ARE YOU DOING, KID?

I THINK THE KING SHOULD FINISH HIS LAST RACE!

YOU JUST GAVE UP THE PISTON CUP, YOU KNOW THAT?

THIS GRUMPY OLD RACE CAR ONCE TOLD ME...

IT'S JUST AN EMPTY CUP!

HEY, WHAT'S GOING ON?

COME ON, BABY! BRING OUT THE PISTON CUP!

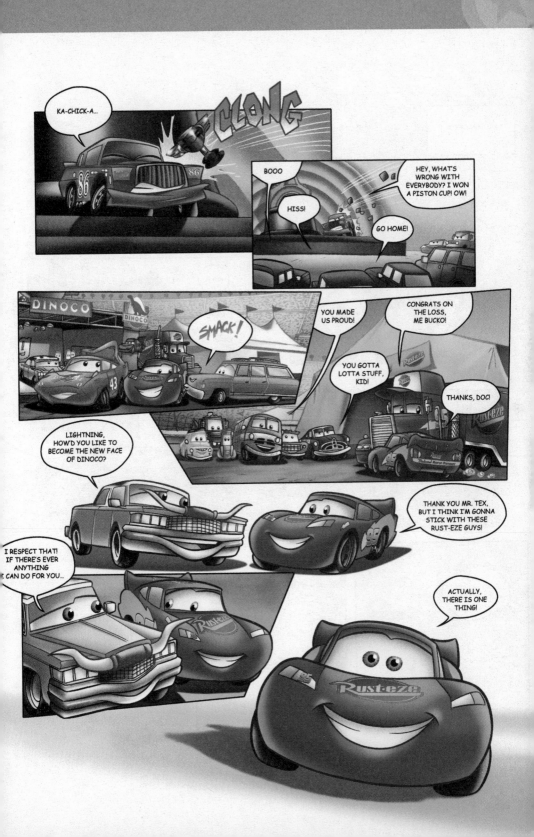

TWO DAYS LATER...

WOO-HOO! LOOK AT ME!

I'M FLYIN'!

HUH?

GASP! A REAL FERRARI IN MY STORE!

LIGHTNING MCQUEEN TOLD ME THIS WAS THE BEST PLACE IN THE WORLD TO GET TIRES!

KA-CHOW!

JUST PASSIN' THROUGH?

I THOUGHT I'D STOP AND STAY AWHILE! I HEAR THIS PLACE IS BACK ON THE MAP!

IT IS?

YEAH! SOME HOT SHOT PISTON CUP RACE CAR IS SETTING UP HIS BIG RACING HEADQUARTERS HERE!

MANY COUNTRIES MIGHT DISPUTE THIS FACT, WE FRENCH KNOW THE TRUTH: THE BEST FOOD IN THE WORLD IS MADE IN FRANCE.

AND THE BEST FOOD IN FRANCE IS MADE IN PARIS!

THE BEST FOOD IN PARIS, SOME SAY, IS MADE BY CHEF AUGUSTE GUSTEAU.

AMUSING TITLE, "*ANYONE CAN COOK!*". WHAT'S EVEN MORE AMUSING IS THAT GUSTEAU ACTUALLY SEEMS TO BELIEVE IT!

GUSTEAU'S RESTAURANT IS THE TOAST OF PARIS. HIS COOKBOOK "*ANYONE CAN COOK!*" IS A BESTSELLER.

ANTON EGO - FOOD CRITIC

BUT IT'S IMPOSSIBLE TO RESIST! THERE ARE SO MANY GOOD THINGS IN THE KITCHEN...

... WONDERFUL!

CLICK

... BUT IT DOESN'T COME WITHOUT ITS DANGERS!

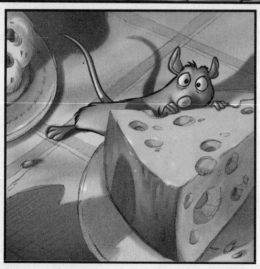

SO REMY HAS A SECRET LIFE FULL OF DANGERS.

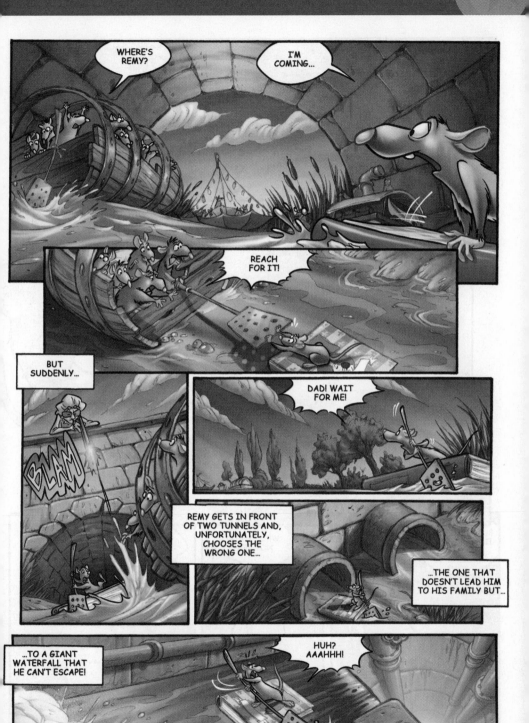

362

NOW REMY'S REALLY IN TROUBLE! WHAT TO DO? HIGHTAIL IT? OR...

WHAT ARE YOU WAITING FOR? YOU KNOW HOW TO FIX IT! THIS IS YOUR CHANCE!

...

SNIFF SNIFF

SWISSSH

WHERE'S THE SOUP... YOU ARE COOKING?!

N-NO!

YOU ARE EITHER LUCKY OR UNLUCKY! YOU WILL MAKE THE SOUP AGAIN AND THIS TIME I'LL BE PAYING VERY CLOSE ATTENTION...

BUT YOU KNOW WHAT I THINK, LINGUINI?

I THINK YOU ARE A SNEAKY, LITTLE...

RAT! RAT! GET IT!

!

NOW WHAT?

KILL IT! IF ANYONE FINDS OUT WE'VE GOT A RAT IN THE KITCHEN, THEY'LL CLOSE US DOWN!

BUT SKINNER IS IN FOR ANOTHER SURPRISE! REMEMBER THE LETTER LINGUINI GAVE HIM?

GET ME MY LAWYER!

SO, A LITTLE WHILE LATER...

GUSTEAU'S WILL STATES THAT IF AFTER FIVE YEARS NO RIGHTFUL HEIR IS FOUND, THE RESTAURANT IS YOURS!

I'M FULLY AWARE OF THAT, TALON! WHAT I WANT TO KNOW IS WHETHER THIS LETTER CHANGES ANYTHING!

HE ARRIVES WITH A LETTER FROM HIS MOTHER CLAIMING GUSTEAU IS HIS FATHER! AND HE DOESN'T KNOW! HIGHLY SUSPECT!

WAS THIS GUSTEAU'S?

I'LL NEED A SAMPLE OF THE BOY'S DNA AS WELL... A HAIR, PERHAPS!

373

DON'T YOU DARE!

SWOP

IT'S HARD TO EXPLAIN...UH... I'M SORRY!

BUT THIS TIME AS WELL, THE DISH IS A BIG SUCCESS!

AND LINGUINI BRINGS OUT HIS FRIEND TO CATCH A BREATH OF AIR...

TAKE A BREAK LITTLE CHEF! WE REALLY DID IT TONIGHT...

LINGUINI GOES BACK TO THE KITCHEN WHERE SKINNER COMES VERY CLOSE TO FINDING OUT THE SECRET...

A-AH?!

SWISS

HEM, I'D LOVE TO TALK WITH YOU IN MY OFFICE! JUST US COOKS!

HE WON'T BE COMING TO YOU FOR ADVICE ANYMORE, COLETTE? HE'S GOTTEN ALL HE NEEDS...

LET US TOAST..

UH, I DON'T REALLY... UH... SURE, OK!

MEANWHILE, REMY IS CELEBRATING WITH A NICE PIECE OF CHEESE WHEN...

MUNCH... MUNCH... ?

RUSTLE

EMILE!

REMY!

I CAN'T BELIEVE IT! YOU'RE ALIVE! YOU MADE IT!

WHAT ARE YOU EATING?

UMM... I DON'T REALLY KNOW! I THINK IT WAS SOME SORT OF WRAPPER ONCE!

YOU'RE IN PARIS, NOW! AND MY BROTHER'S NOT GOING TO BE EATING GARBAGE IN MY TOWN!

REMY GOES TO THE FOOD VAULT OF THE RESTAURANT, AND...

YOU ARE STEALING?

IT'S JUST THIS ONCE! IT'S FOR MY BROTHER... JUST THIS ONCE...

375

IN THE MEANTIME, REMY IS BACK AT HOME...

MY SON HAS RETURNED!

HURRAAAHHH

HURRAAAH

IT HASN'T BEEN EASY... FINDING SOMEONE TO REPLACE YOU FOR POISON CHECKER HAS BEEN A DISASTER!

WELL...

THE IMPORTANT THING IS YOU'RE HOME! IT'S TOUGH OUT THERE, ISN'T IT?

SURE... BUT I'VE FOUND A NICE SPOT NOT FAR AWAY...

WHAT'S THAT SON?

IT'S NOT LIKE I'M A KID ANYMORE, DAD! NOW I CAN TAKE CARE OF MYSELF!

AND I'LL BE ABLE TO VISIT OFTEN...

YOU ARE NOT STAYING?

YOU DIDN'T THINK I WAS GOING TO STAY FOREVER, DID YOU?

EVENTUALLY A BIRD'S GOTTA LEAVE THE NEST!

WE'RE NOT BIRDS, WE'RE RATS!

WELL, MAYBE I'M A DIFFERENT KIND OF RAT!

MAYBE YOU'RE NOT A RAT AT ALL!

MAYBE THAT'S A GOOD THING! I'M TIRED OF TAKING! I WANT TO MAKE THINGS!

YOU'RE TALKING LIKE A HUMAN...

... WHO ARE NOT AS BAD AS YOU SAY!

OH, YEAH? COME WITH ME... THERE'S SOMETHING I WANT YOU TO SEE!

HERE WE ARE...

... AT THE SAME INSTANT, INSIDE THE POWERFUL FOOD CRITIC ANTON EGO'S HOUSE, THE SURPRISES BEGIN...

GUSTEAU'S PLACE... IT'S COME BACK. IT'S POPULAR, MR. EGO!

WHAT? MY LAST REVIEW CONDEMNED IT TO THE TOURIST TRADE!

THEN TELL ME, AMBRISTER... HOW COULD IT BE "POPULAR"?

AND AS FOR SKINNER? THERE'S A SURPRISE FOR HIM, TOO...

NO! NO! NOOO!

THE DNA MATCHES! HE IS GUSTEAU'S SON!

THIS CAN'T JUST HAPPEN! THE WHOLE THING IS A SET-UP!

...BUT UNFORTUNATELY WE KNOW HE'S GOT SOMETHING UP HIS SLEEVE... TROUBLE FOR REMY COMING!

ACTUALLY IT LOOKS AS IF REMY'S ALREADY IN TROUBLE!

YOU TOLD THEM? THAT'S EXACTLY WHAT I SAID NOT TO DO!

BUT THEY'RE... MY FRIENDS... I'M SORRY...

JUST LET US IN, AND WE CAN...

NO... WAIT HERE! AND STAY OUT OF SIGHT!

REMY DECIDES TO FEED EMILE'S FRIENDS BUT THE DOOR TO THE FOOD VAULT IS LOCKED...

REMY, WHAT ARE YOU DOING IN HERE?

EMILE... I SAID NOT TO BUT... ANYWAY, THEY ARE HUNGRY AND I NEED THE KEY!

OH, HERE IT IS! HEY... YOUR WILL AND A LETTER FROM LINGUINI'S MOTHER!

LINGUINI... HE'S YOUR SON?! HOW COULD YOU NOT KNOW THIS?

I'M A FIGMENT OF YOUR IMAGINATION! YOU DID NOT KNOW... HOW COULD I?

CREAK

HE IS A CRITIC! THE TOP CRITIC! HE'S GOING TO REVIEW US AGAIN...

OH, WELL! BRING IT ON! HIS TASTE BUDS WILL BE BEGGING FOR MERCY WHEN WE'RE FINISHED WITH HIM!

LINGUINI IS OVER-CONFIDENT AND REMY DISAPPROVES THE BEHAVIOR...

YANK

YOU TAKE A BREAK, LITTLE CHEF! I'M NOT A PUPPET!

GASP! THE RAT... IS THE COOK!

THAT EVENING, IN THE KITCHEN, LINGUINI WANTS TO MAKE UP...

...BUT DISCOVERS THAT REMY HAS LET THE OTHER RATS ENTER IN THE KITCHEN AS SPITE!

LITTLE CHEF? YOU'RE HERE?

HERE YOU ARE... LOOK, I DON'T WANT TO FIGHT!

YOU'VE NEVER FAILED ME, AND I SHOULD NEVER FORGET THAT...

OOF!

WHAT IS THIS? YOU'RE STEALING FROM ME! I THOUGHT YOU WERE MY FRIEND!

GET OUT! YOU AND ALL YOUR RAT BUDDIES AND DON'T COME BACK, PESTS!

AND ONCE OUT IN THE STREET...

YOU ARE RIGHT, DAD! WHO AM I KIDDING...

WE ARE WHAT WE ARE! AND WE ARE RATS! YOU KNOW HOW TO GET IN... STEAL ALL YOU WANT...

NEXT DAY...

JUST CAN'T LEAVE IT ALONE, CAN'T YOU?

WHAT ARE YOU DOING HERE DURING RESTAURANT'S HOURS? IT'S NOT SAFE!

I'M HUNGRY! AND I DON'T NEED THE INSIDE FOOD TO BE HAPPY... OBSERVE!

NO, WAIT!

!

OH, NO! WHAT DO WE DO? I'LL GO GET DAD!

NO, IT'S OKAY! IT'S JUST LINGUINI TRYING TO MAKE A POINT! HE'LL LET ME GO ONCE HE...

TUMP

BUT...

YOU MIGHT BE CLEVER, BUT YOU'RE STILL ONLY A RAT!

ONCE GOT RID OF REMY, SKINNER ENTERS IN THE RESTAURANT TO GLOAT OVER LINGUINI'S DEFEAT.

.. WHILE REMY IS LOCKED IN THE TRUNK OF HIS CAR!

WE ARE IN A CAGE...

NO, I'M THE ONE IN A CAGE! I'VE GIVEN UP! YOU ARE FREE...

I'M ONLY AS FREE AS YOU IMAGINE ME TO BE! AS YOU ARE...

OH, PLEASE, I'M SICK OF PRETENDING! I PRETEND TO BE A RAT FOR MY FATHER! TO BE HUMAN THROUGH LINGUINI...

I KNOW WHO I AM! WHY DO I NEED TO PRETEND?

AH, BUT YOU DON'T, REMY... YOU DON'T...

BUT DJANGO IS COMING TO THE RESCUE: THE RATS ARE PUSHING A GARGOYLE OFF THE ROOF...

PUSH! COME ON!

SSCRRRAPE

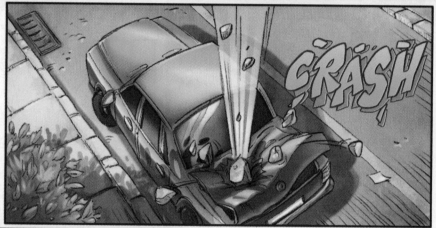

CRASH

HEY, LITTLE BROTHER!

SOON REMY IS FREE! BUT NOW WHAT? RUN OR...

... GO BACK?

QUICK! TO THE RESTAURANT!

I KNOW THIS SOUNDS INSANE... BUT THE TRUTH SOUNDS INSANE, SOMETIMES!

AND THE TRUTH IS I HAVE NO TALENT AT ALL! BUT THIS RAT... HE IS THE REAL COOK!

HE IS CONTROLLING MY ACTIONS! THIS RAT, THIS BRILLIANT LITTLE CHEF CAN LEAD US...

YANK

WHADDYA SAY? YOU WITH ME?

NO, LINGUINI! NO ONE CAN ACCEPT THE IDEA OF REMY COOKING... NOT EVEN COLETTE...

SIGH..

BUT SOMEONE ELSE HAS DECIDED TO PUT HIS FAITH IN REMY!

YOU'VE STOOD BY HIM! I'M PROUD OF YOU!

NOW... WE'RE NOT COOKS, BUT YOU TELL US WHAT TO DO...

"... AND WE'LL GET IT DONE!"

... TEAM THREE WILL BE HANDLING FISH!

TEAM FOUR, ROASTED ITEMS! GO GO GO!

SPLASH

FRIZZLE

WE NEED SOMEONE TO WAIT TABLES...

AND LINGUINI UNDERSTANDS HE'S THE ONE WHO CAN DO THIS... WITH HIS ROLLER SKATES!

I'M SORRY FOR ANY DELAY, BUT WE'RE A LITTLE SHORT TONIGHT!

EH, EH! PLEASE, TAKE ALL THE TIME YOU NEED!

UNTIL...

COLETTE? OH, YOU CAME BACK!

DON'T SAY A WORD! JUST TELL ME WHAT THE RAT WANTS TO COOK!

RATATOUILLE? THIS DISH IS HUMBLE... EGO IS NOT! ARE YOU SURE YOU WANT TO SERVE THIS TO HIM?

WELL, I'LL HELP YOU ANYWAY!

?

YOU WANT TO PUT THOSE IN INSTEAD?

AT LAST, THE DISH ARRIVES AT TERRIBLE EGO'S TABLE...

RATATOUILLE? THEY MUST BE JOKING!

EGO SNIFFS...

HE TASTES...

AND IS LITERALLY ENTHRALLED! WHO IS RESPONSIBLE FOR SUCH AN EXQUISITE DISH?

I'M JUST YOUR WAITER, TONIGHT...

THEN WHO DO I THANK FOR THE MEAL?

...SO HE DEMANDS TO MEET THE MYSTERY CHEF! COLETTE AND LINGUINI AGREE, BUT ONLY IF EGO WAITS UNTIL THE OTHER DINERS HAVE GONE!

"AND FINALLY THEY BRING ME OUT!"

"THE FOLLOWING DAY, HIS REVIEW APPEARS..."

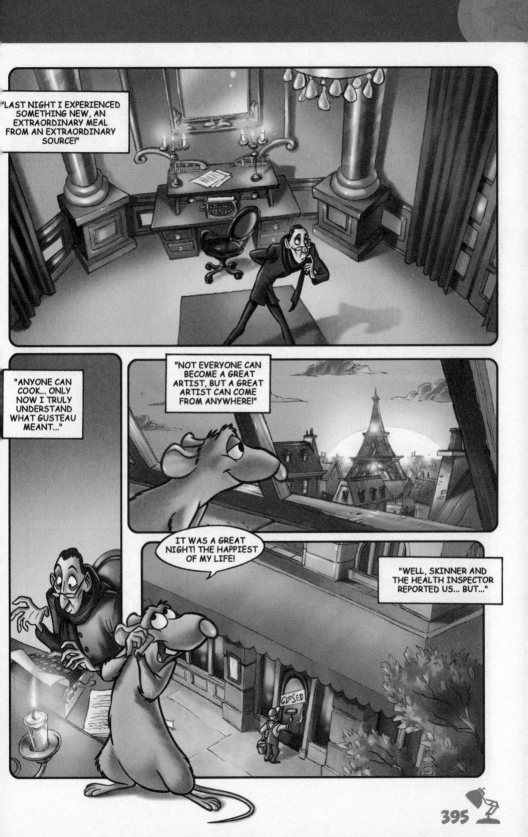

395

... BUT... GOTTA GO! DINNER RUSH!

TINK TINK

IH, IH!

EH, EH! IT SEEMS THE CHEF IS LATE!

EH, EH!

YOU KNOW HOW HE LIKES IT...

THANK YOU, LITTLE CHEF!

HERE IT IS!

CAN I INTEREST YOU IN A DESSERT, THIS EVENING?

DON'T YOU ALWAYS?

SURPRISE ME!

HERE ENDS THE STORY OF REMY! BUT IT'S JUST THE BEGINNING FOR A NEW RESTAURANT IN TOWN...

THAT STORY GETS EVEN BETTER WHEN I TELL IT!

A VERY SPECIAL RESTAURANT, WITH ONE HECK OF A GREAT LITTLE CHEF!

THE END

WHRRR

KLUDD

Wool

Hmm...

Ah!

TA-DAH!

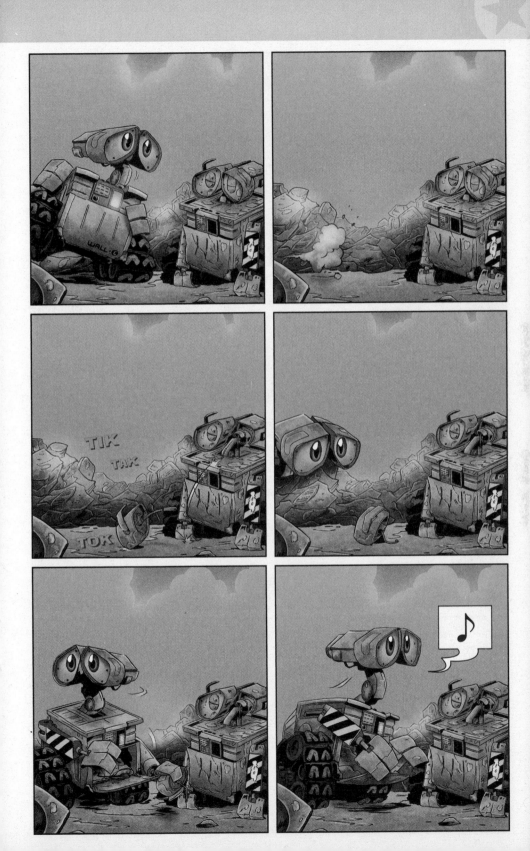

sigh

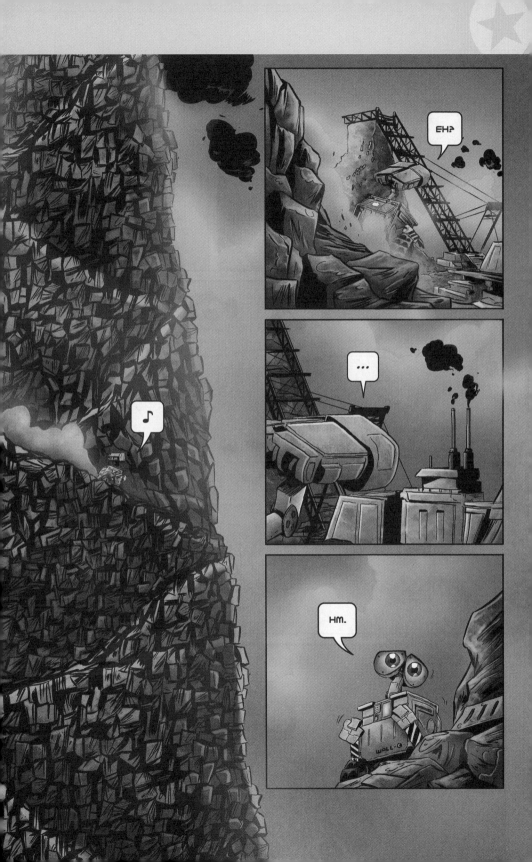

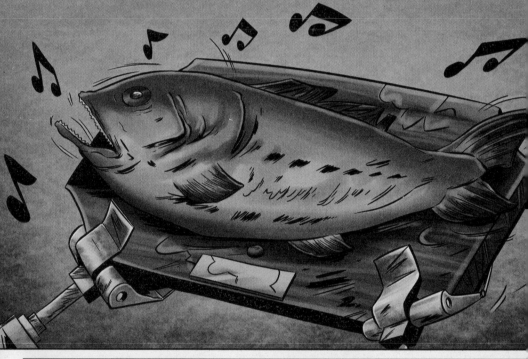

KLUDD

UH-OH.

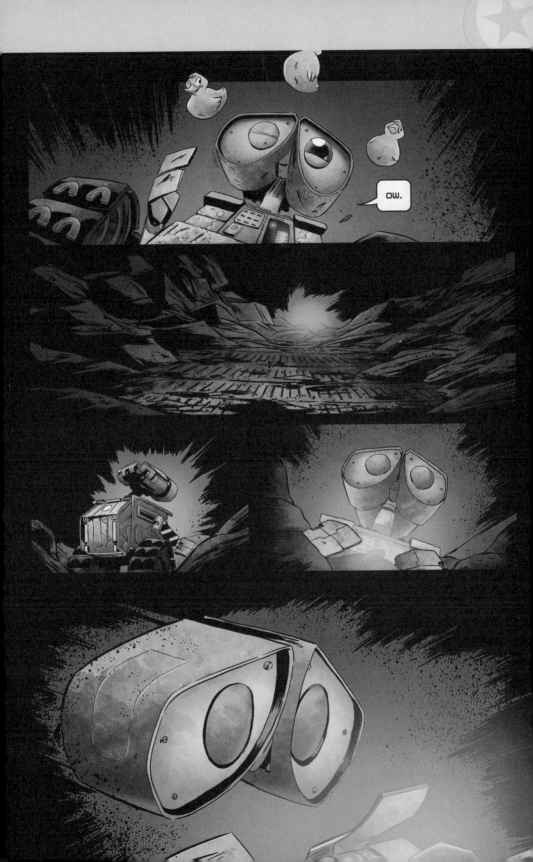

NNN...

...OH.

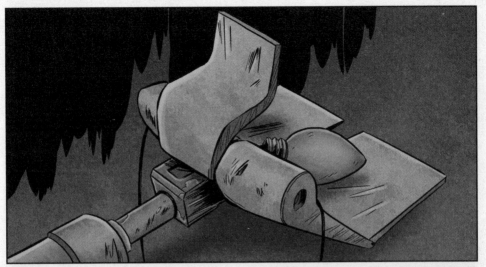

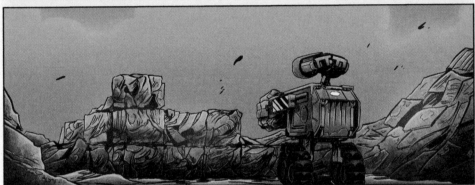

HM.

HUH?

OH.

KRIK

KRAK

KRRRUNCH

WEEEEE!

NEH...

NEH!

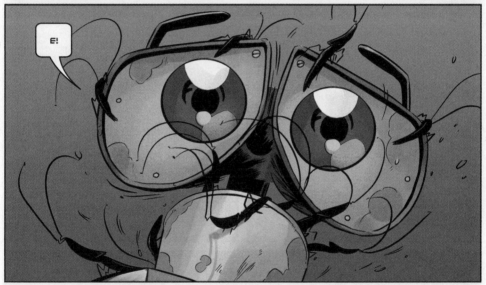

E!

WHARRR!

NEH!

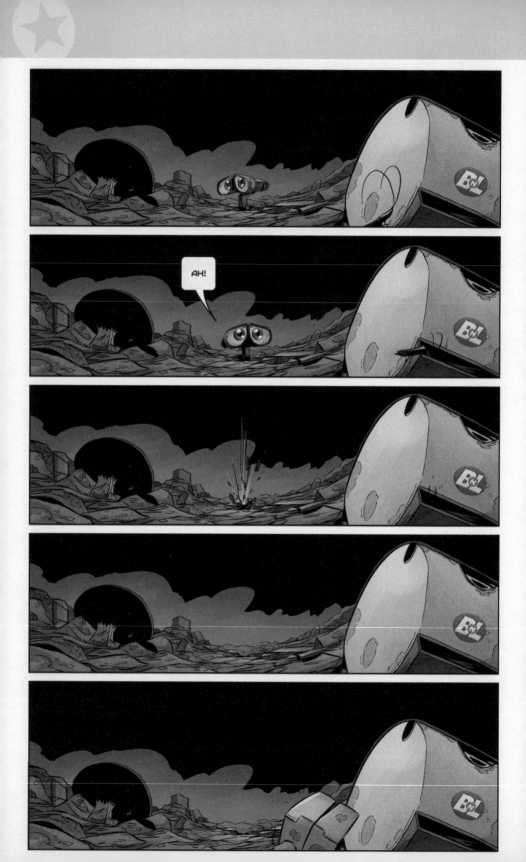

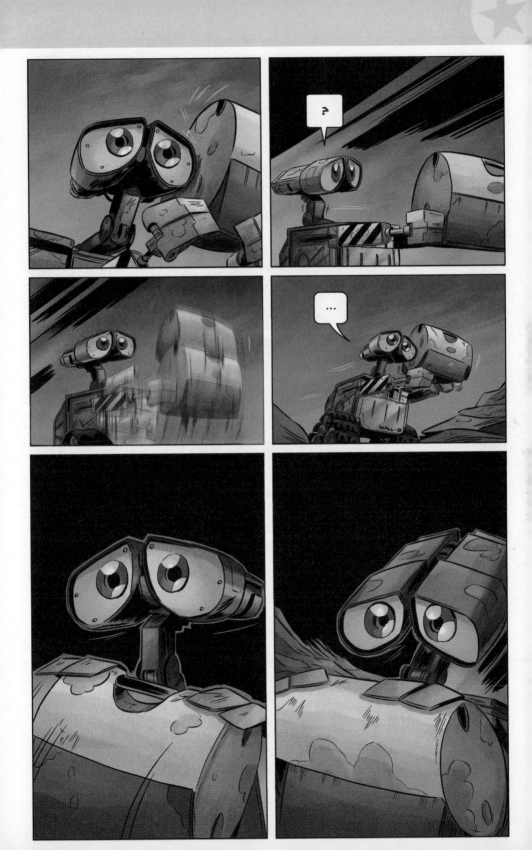

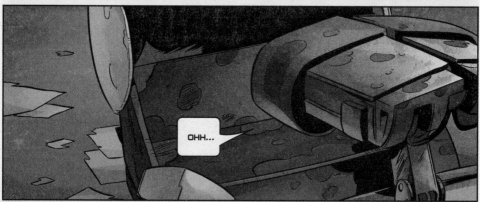

OHH...

WHRRRRRRRRRRRRRR

KLUDD

SIGH.

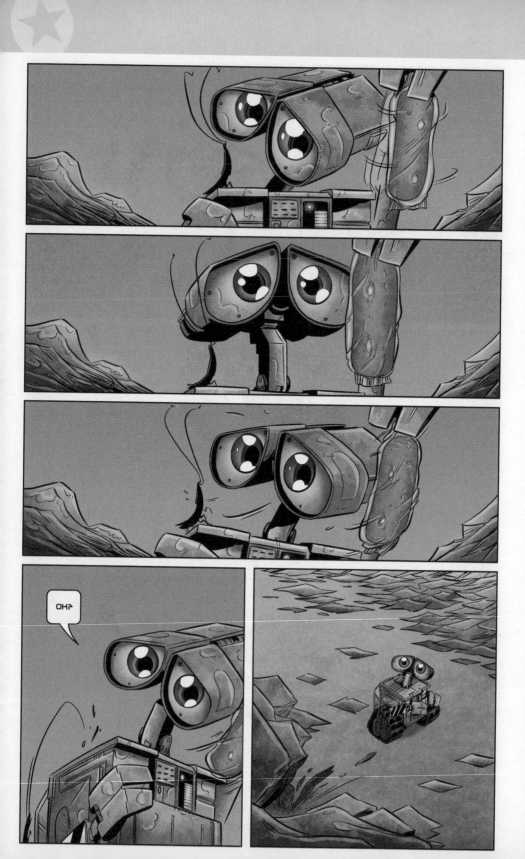

KLUNK

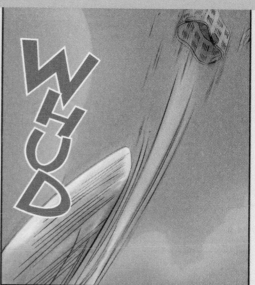

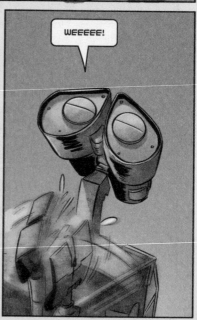

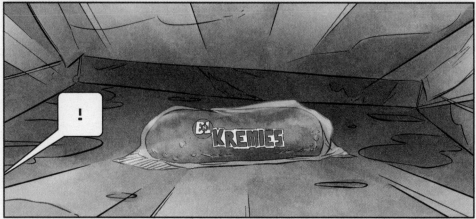

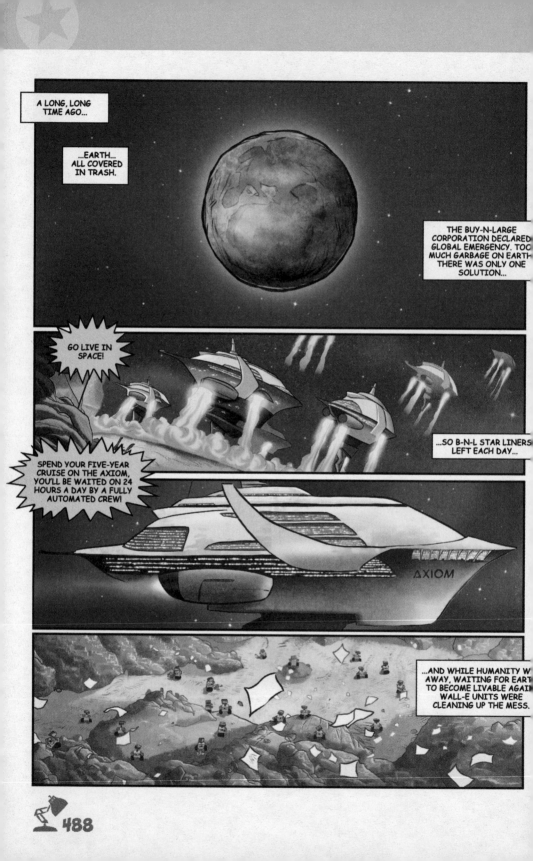

EARTH.

NOW.

STILL A DRAB AND BROWN PLANET.

THE SURFACE, MOUNTAINS, CITIES, SKYSCRAPERS... EVERYTHING IS STILL COVERED IN TRASH.

AND SOMEONE IS STILL CUBING IT.

AFTER 700 YEARS...

TRRRTRRR

VzzzCLACK

STOMP

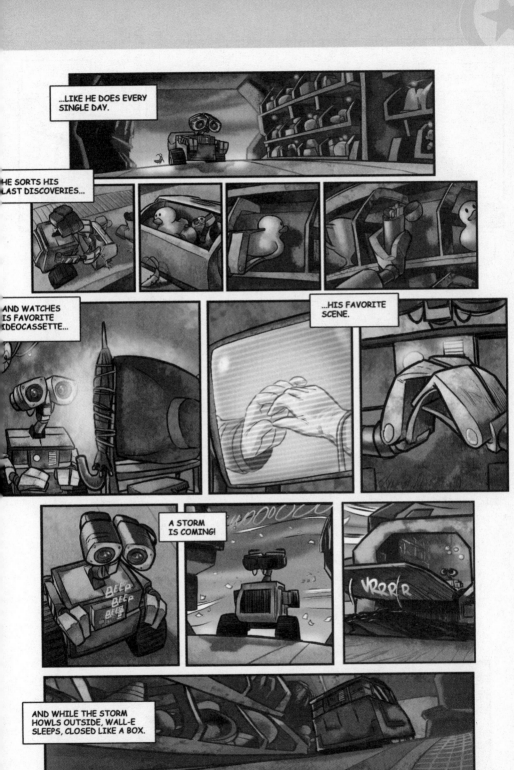

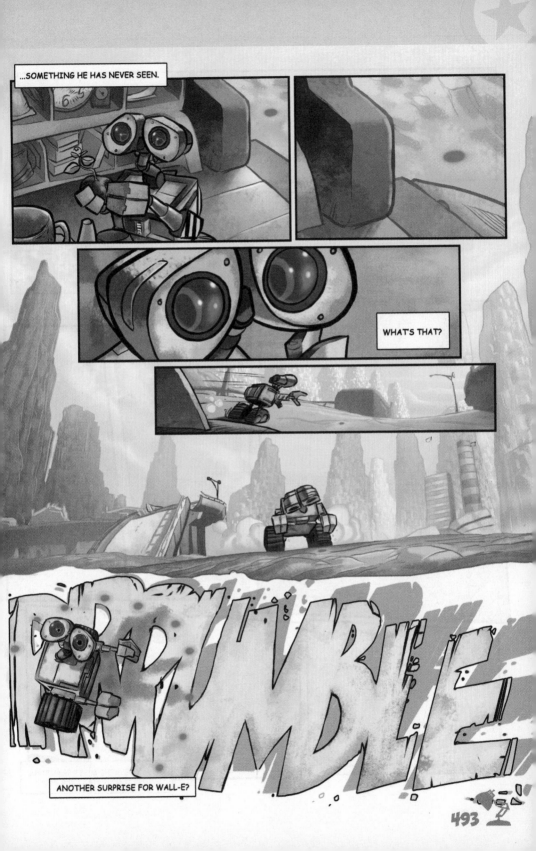

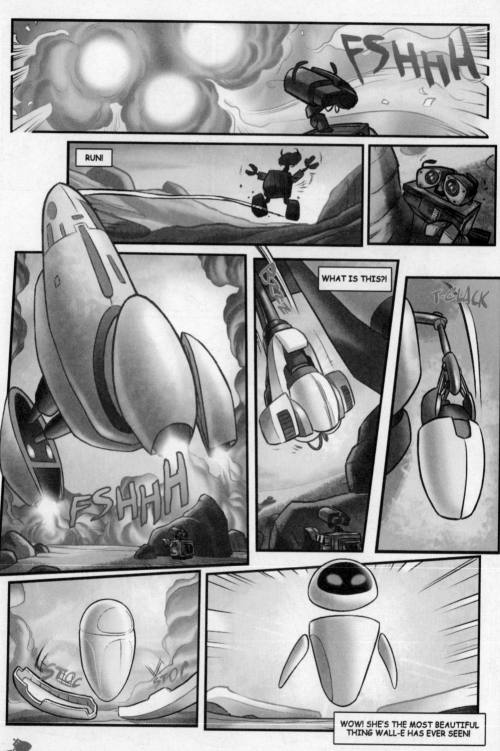

AFTER MANY DAYS, SHE GIVES UP.

AND WALL-E TIMIDLY GETS CLOSER.

WHO ARE YOU?

W-WALLEEE? ...WALLEEE!

WWWAAALEEE...?

WALLEEE.

EVE.

EEEE...? EEEAAAH?

EEEVE. EEEVE.

EEE-VAH!

EEE-VAH!

HEE HEE!

BEEP BEEP

A SAND STORM IS COMING!

NOOOOOOOOo

WALL-E TAKES EVE TO A SAFE PLACE... HOME...

...AND SHOWS HER ALL HIS DISCOVERIES!

A LIGHT BULB...

OOOH!

...A LIGHTER...

FHSSS

...AND THE MOST PRECIOUS ONE.

EE-VAH!

BUT WALL-E'S TREASURE...

BZZZ

...IS EXACTLY WHAT EVE'S BEEN LOOKING FOR!

ZZZWWW

CRRR CLICK

EE-VAH?

SHE DOESN'T ANSWER.

EE-VAH? EE-VAH?

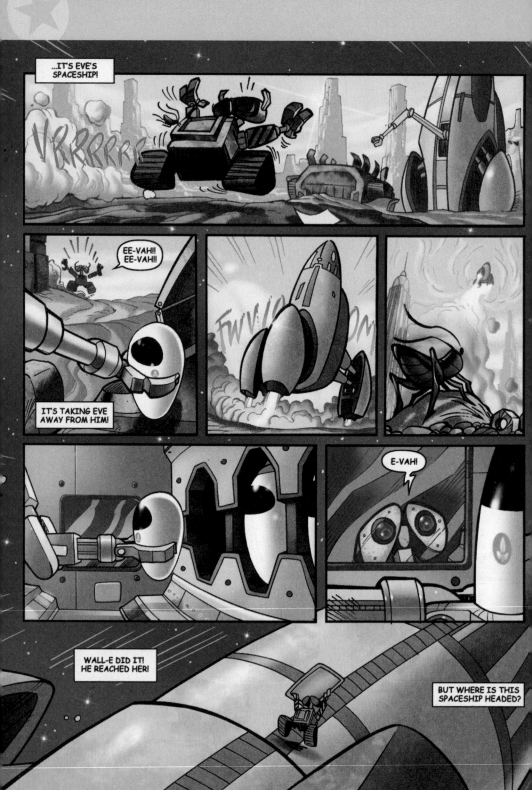

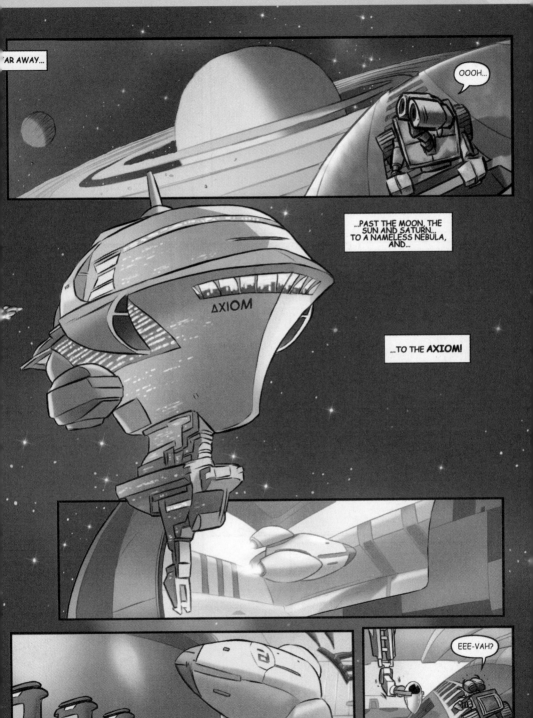

EVE IS LOWERED FROM THE SPACESHIP FOR THE ANALYSIS...

...OF THE CLEANER BOT M-O!

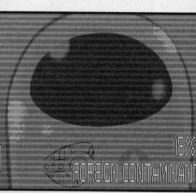

15%
FOREIGN CONTAMINANT

SO MUCH DIRT! HE HAS TO CLEAN HER IMMEDIATELY!

FRRR
FRRR
FRRR

BZZZ

WHO IS THIS?

BZZZ

M-O'S NEVER SEEN ANYTHING SO FILTHY.

!

1833%
FOREIGN CONTAMINANT

FRRR
FRRR
FRRR

BUT WALL-E DOESN'T WANT TO BE CLEANED.

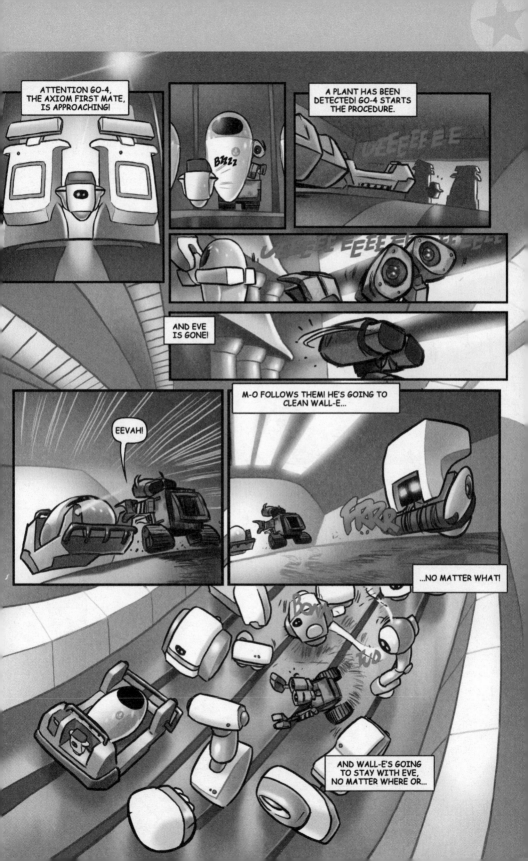

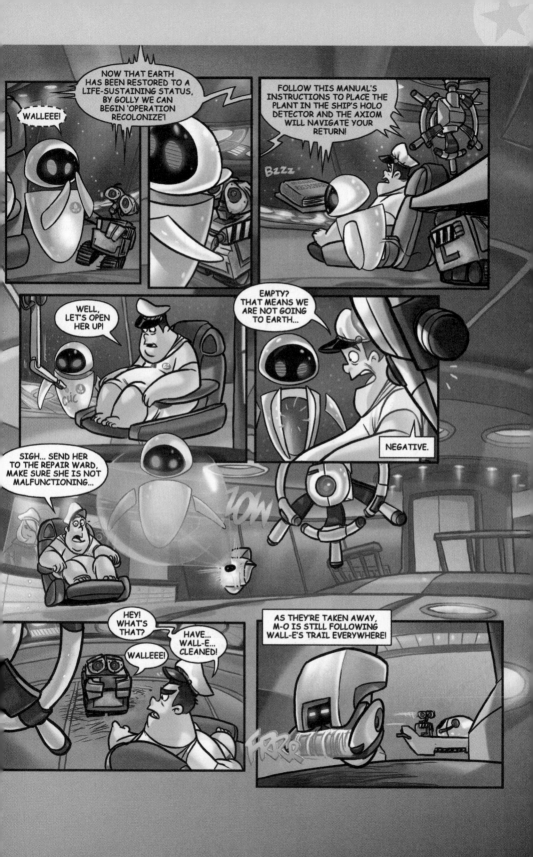

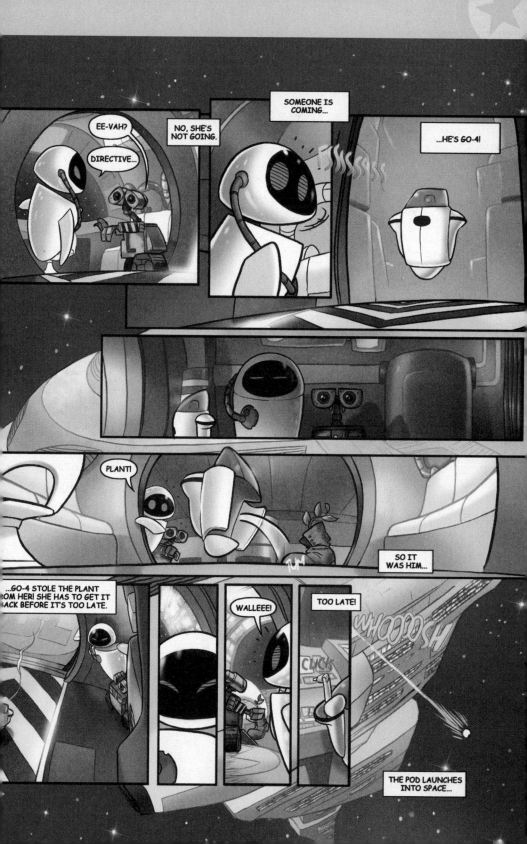

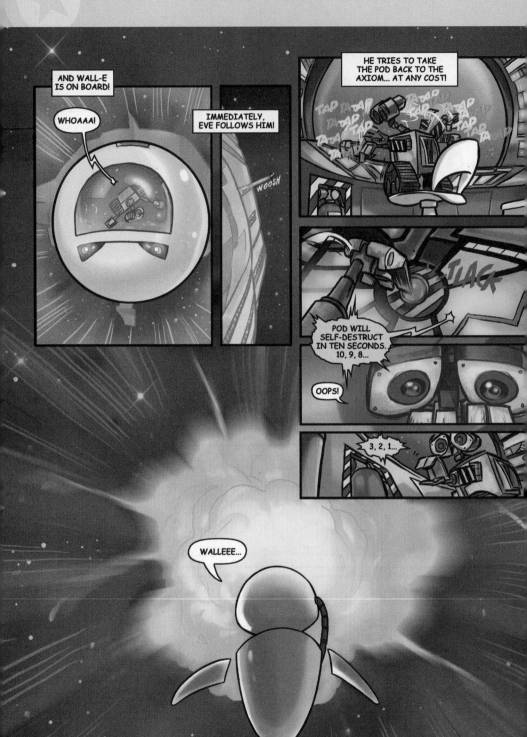

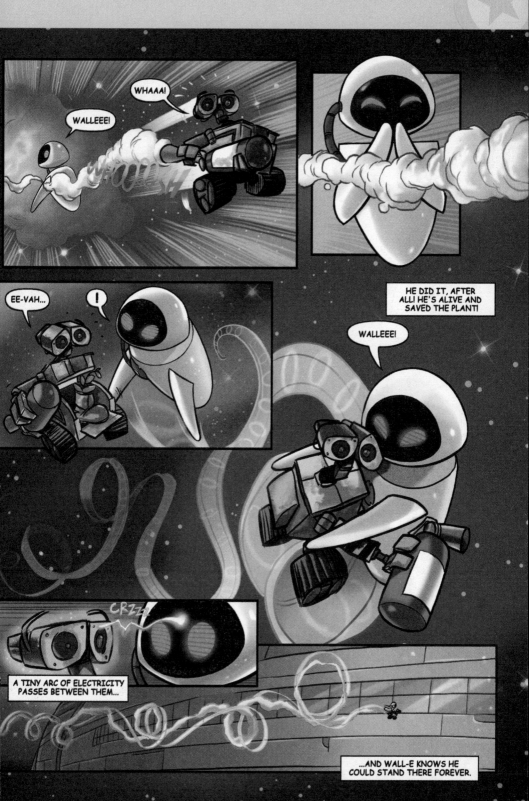

AND WHILE THE CAPTAIN LOOKS AFTER THE LITTLE PLANT...

...EVE COMES ACROSS SOMETHING UNEXPECTED IN HER MEMORY IMAGES.

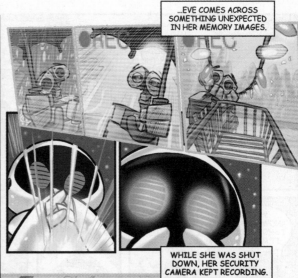

THERE. YOU COME A LONG WAY FOR A DRINK OF WATER...

WHILE SHE WAS SHUT DOWN, HER SECURITY CAMERA KEPT RECORDING.

AND NOW, LOOKING AT IT, SHE REALIZES...

...THE MEANING OF WALL-E'S LOVE.

HE'S STILL WAITING FOR HER. SHE HAS TO LEAVE IMMEDIATELY AND GO BACK TO...

AUTO!

AUTO, EVE FOUND THE PLANT! WE'RE GOING HOME. FIRE UP THE HOLO-DETECTOR!

NOT NECESSARY, CAPTAIN. YOU MAY GIVE IT TO ME.

YOU KNOW WHAT, I SHOULD DO IT MYSELF!

SIR, I INSIST YOU GIVE ME THE PLANT.

AUTO, GET OUT OF MY WAY!

SIR, WE CANNOT GO HOME.

WHAT ARE YOU TALKING ABOUT? WHY NOT?

THIS IS CLASSIFIED. GIVE ME THE PLANT.

"CLASSIFIED"? YOU DON'T KEEP SECRETS FROM THE CAPTAIN. TELL ME EVERYTHING! THAT'S AN ORDER!

AYE-AYE, SIR.

HEY THERE, AUTOPILOTS! GOT SOME BAD NEWS. OPERATION CLEAN-UP HAS, UH, WELL... FAILED! LIFE ON EARTH IS UNSUSTAINABLE...

UNSUSTAINABLE? WHAT?

WE HAVE TO CANCEL OPERATION RECOLONIZE. GO TO FULL AUTOPILOT. TAKE CONTROL OF EVERYTHING! AND DO NOT RETURN TO EARTH!

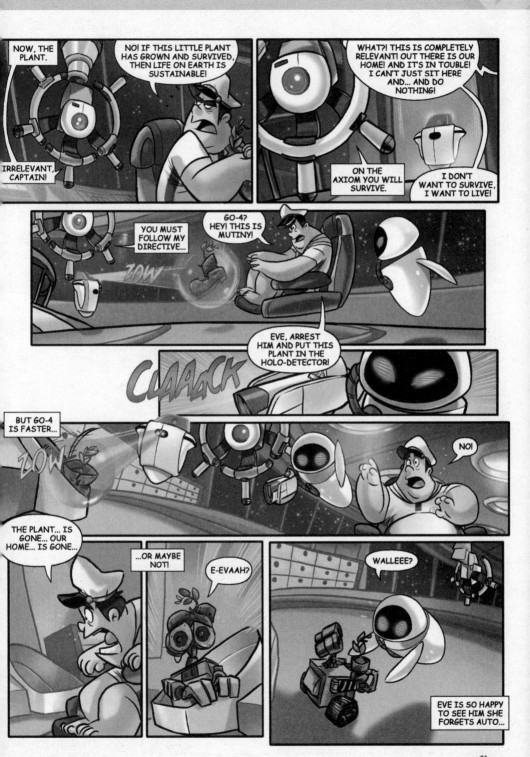

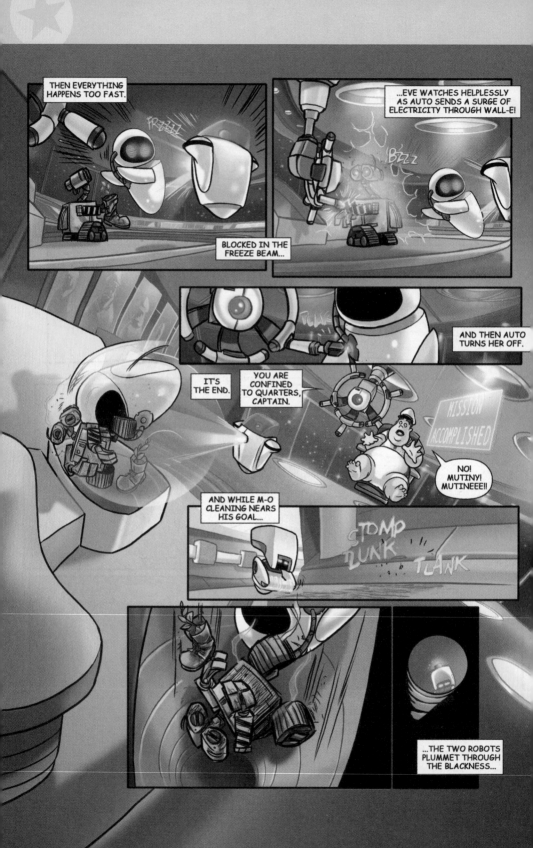

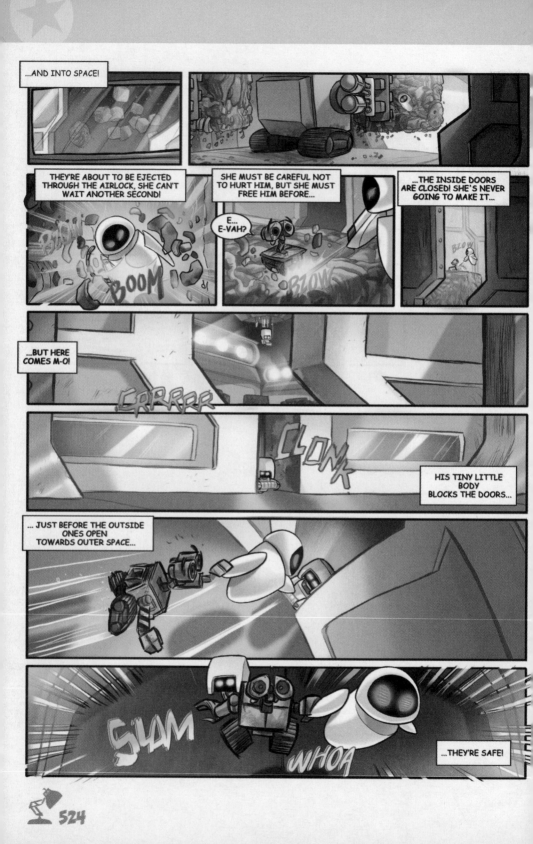

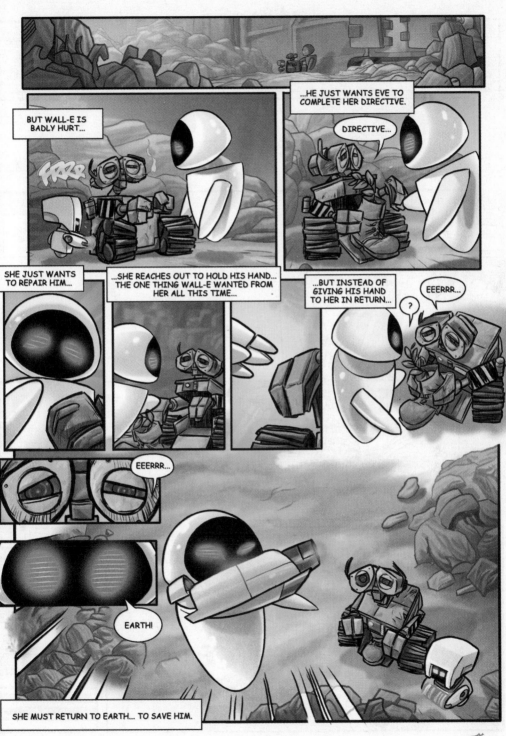

...GOTCHA! HA HA!

CLK

SUDDENLY, KLAXONS SOUND ALL OVER THE SHIP, THE LIDO DECK POOLS ARE COVERED UP AND EVERY HOVER CHAIR HEADS OFF IN THE SAME DIRECTION!

HEY, CHAIR! WHERE ARE WE GOING? CHAIR?

LOOK!

THE HOLO-DETECTOR IS ACTIVATING! EVE AND WALL-E SWOOP IN WITH THE PLANT.

VZZZ

ENOUGH!

WOOOAH!

CRLRLRL

TUMP

BUT AUTO FURIOUSLY SPINS HIS WHEEL...

...AND THE ENTIRE SHIP LISTS DANGEROUSLY TO ONE SIDE!

WAAAH!

WOOOOOOOO

EVERYONE FALLS...

...EVERYTHING FALLS...

SBAM

AUTO PUSHES THE BUTTON ONCE MORE.

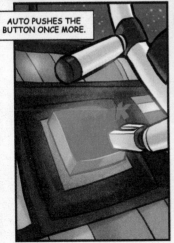

THE HOLO-DETECTOR IS CLOSING AND NO ONE CAN STOP IT.

!

...HE REAWAKENS!

BOING BOING

DING♪

WALLEEE...

HE GIVES HER A BLANK STARE AND TURNS AWAY FROM HER... SOMETHING'S WRONG.

EVE!

HE DOESN'T SEEM TO KNOW WHO SHE IS...

...HE JUST CUBES.

NO.

TRRRTRRR

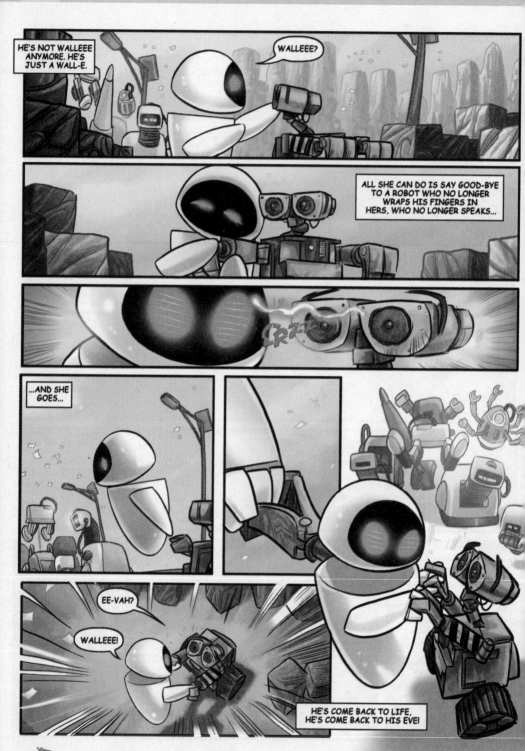

AND SO IT IS A HAPPY ENDING FOR WALL-E AND EVE...

.AND EVERYONE IS AFFECTED BY ONE LITTLE ROBOT'S DESIRE...

...TO FOLLOW HIS HEART.

THE·END

TSK! RETIREMENT VILLAGE, OH, BROTHER.

HEY, **TOM!** YOU BOYS ARE STIRRING UP QUITE A DUST BOWL HERE!

LOOK, MR. FREDRICKSEN... IT'S NONE OF MY BUSINESS BUT, UH, YOU CAN'T BE HAPPY HERE.

WHY DON'T YOU JUST SELL THE PLACE?

I'VE MADE MY POSITION CLEAR, TOM. I WON'T LEAVE.

HE DOESN'T WANT ANYTHING TO DISTURB HIS LIFE...

NEVER, ELLIE.

KNOCK KNOCK

?

I'LL FIND IT, MR. FREDRICKSEN!

I THINK ITS BURROW IS TWO BLOCKS DOWN!

HEH-HEH!

BAM

WHAT? HEY, YOU!

I'M SORRY, SIR. LET ME TAKE CARE OF IT FOR YOU.

GET AWAY FROM OUR MAILBOX!

THAT'S MUCH MORE THAN A SIMPLE MAILBOX TO CARL.

IT'S ELLIE'S MEMORY AND HE'S JUST TRYING TO PROTECT IT...

POW

I DON'T WANT YOU TO TOUCH IT!

OW!

I'M SORRY! I DIDN'T... I DIDN'T MEAN TO...

THE NEXT MORNING, WHEN CARL WAKES UP, EVERYTHING IS OVER...

HUH... WHA...WHAT HAPPENED?

AFTER YOU TIED YOUR STUFF DOWN, YOU TOOK A **NAP**, SO I WENT AHEAD AND **STEERED US DOWN** HERE...

TOO MUCH FOG! CAN'T TELL **WHERE WE ARE**...

BUT SUDDENLY...

WE CAN'T BE CLOSE TO THE GROUND.

BAM

AAARGH!

!

THE NEXT MORNING A LOUD SOUND WAKES UP CARL AND RUSSEL...

HAR! HAR!

HAR! HAR!

WHAT IS IT DOING?

THE BIRD IS CALLING **HER** BABIES.

KEVIN'S A **GIRL**?

HAR! HAR!

THE BABIES ARE **ANSWERING** HER!

HAR! HAR!

SHE MUST GET BACK TO THEM. HER HOUSE IS IN THOSE **TWISTY** ROCKS...

I UNDERSTAND... YOU HAVE TO GO...

RUSSELL FEELS LIKE HE'S JUST LOST A FRIEND.

IT'S REALLY **HIM!** MY NAME IS CARL FREDRICKSEN. MY WIFE AND I WERE YOUR BIGGEST **FANS!**

IS THAT SO? WELL, COME ON **IN!**

Spirit of Adven

YOU MUST BE TIRED. **HUNGRY.**

WOW, WE'RE ACTUALLY GOING INSIDE THE **"SPIRIT OF ADVENTURE"** ITSELF!

NOT YOU.

HE HAS LOST THE BIRD. PUT HIM IN THE **CONE OF SHAME.**

MOMENTS LATER...

I CAN'T BELIEVE I'M ACTUALLY HERE!

SIGH.

I SEE YOU LIKE MY COLLECTION. THIS... COMFORTS ME, AS THE YEARS PASS. A REMINDER OF WHO I AM.

THEY CALLED ME A FRAUD, THOSE...**BAH!** BUT I KNOW MY NAME WILL BE **CLEARED...**

?!
THEY'RE GONE!

GET THEM!

GET THEM! GET THEM!

FINISH THEM!

HURRY!

I AM HURRYING!

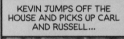

KEVIN JUMPS OFF THE HOUSE AND PICKS UP CARL AND RUSSELL...

DUG TRIES TO HELP THEM ESCAPE...

GO ON, **MASTER!** I'LL STOP THE DOGS!

GRRR

WOOF

WOOF

...BUT THERE ARE TOO MANY DOGS!

BAM

MEANWHILE...

YOU LOST THEM?

DUG **HELPED** THEM ESCAPE! WE SAW HIM GOING AWAY WITH THEM!

WAIT. WAIT A MINUTE. **DUG**...

MUNTZ ACTIVATES THE **TRACKING DEVICE** ON DUG'S COLLAR...

YOU KNOW WHAT? THE [WI]LDERNESS IS NOT QUITE HOW THEY [M]ADE IT SOUND IN MY **BOOK**.

MY DAD AND I, WHEN HE USED TO LIVE WITH US, WE USED TO GET ICE CREAM TOGETHER...

GET USED TO THAT, KID.

...THEN WE'D SIT OUTSIDE FENTON'S, AND I'D COUNT ALL THE BLUE CARS WHILE HE COUNTED THE RED ONES, AND WHOEVER GOT THE MOST WON.

THAT MIGHT SOUND BORING, BUT I THINK THE **BORING STUFF** IS THE STUFF I REMEMBER THE **MOST**.

THE GROUP WALKS SOME TIME IN SILENCE, UNTIL...

LOOK, THERE IT IS! KEVIN'S HOME!

KEVIN! YOU'RE FEELING BETTER, AREN'T YOU?

THAT'S IT. GO, KEVIN. GO FIND YOUR BABIES!

BUT JUST WHEN EVERYTHING SEEMS TO BE OK...

IT'S MUNTZ'S DIRIGIBLE!

WOK WOK WOK WOK

RUN, KEVIN, RUN!

SWISH

HAR!! HAR!!

PFOK

OH, NO!

GET AWAY FROM MY BIRD!

IF YOU WANT YOUR HOUSE BACK.

NO! OUR HOUSE!

CARL IS SORRY FOR KEVIN, BUT HE CAN'T LET IT GO...

LET HER GO! KEVIIIIIN!

CAREFUL. WE'LL WANT HER IN GOOD SHAPE FOR MY RETURN.

HARRR! HARRR!

YOU GAVE KEVIN AWAY! YOU JUST GAVE HER AWAY!

THIS IS NONE OF MY CONCERN! I DIDN'T ASK FOR ANY OF THIS! AND NOW, WHETHER YOU ASSIST ME OR NOT...

"...I AM GOING TO PARADISE FALLS EVEN IF IT KILLS ME."

I DID IT.

HERE. I DON'T WANT THIS ANYMORE.

BAM

THEN, FOR THE FIRST TIME SINCE HE ARRIVED IN SOUTH AMERICA, CARL GOES INSIDE...

HE PICKS ELLIE'S ADVENTURE BOOK UP AND, FOR THE FIRST TIME IN HIS LIFE, HE TURNS TO THE "**STUFF I'M GONNA DO**" PAGES...

...FINDING OUT THEY ARE **NOT BLANK** ANYMORE.

CARL SMILES AND THINKS ABOUT HIS PROMISE. "CROSS MY HEART" HE SAID TO RUSSELL.

hanks for the adventure.

now go have a new one.

Love,

Ellie

THAT'S IT! HER BEST ADVENTURE WAS HER **EVERYDAY LIFE** WITH HIM.

RUSSELL?

FWOOO

I'M GONNA **HELP** KEVIN EVEN IF YOU WON'T!

NO! RUSSELL!

THERE'S NOT A MOMENT TO LOSE! CARL GETS RID OF THINGS IN THE HOUSE, MAKING IT LIFT...

...MAKING IT FL AGAIN!

WAHOOO!

!!!

KNOCK KNOCK

AND AGAIN, SOMEONE IS KNOCKING AT THE DOOR!

DUG!

I WAS HIDING UNDER YOUR PORCH BECAUSE I LOVE YOU. CAN I STAY?

OF COURSE! YOU'RE **MY** DOG!

576

581

Disney · PIXAR

TOY STORY 3

589

WHO ARE WE KIDDIN'? THE KID'S **17** YEARS OLD!

BUT WE CAN TRY AGAIN, RIGHT?

NO, REX. ANDY'S GOING TO COLLEGE ANY DAY NOW... THAT WAS OUR **LAST SHOT**.

WE'RE GOING INTO ATTIC MODE, FOLKS. TAKE ANYTHING YOU NEED FOR AN ORDERLY TRANSITION.

ORDERLY? DON'T YOU GET IT? WE'RE DONE! FINISHED! OVER THE HILL!

WE'RE GETTING **THROWN** AWAY?

WE'RE BEING **ABANDONED**?

WE'LL BE FINE, JESSIE. ANDY IS GONNA TUCK US IN THE ATTIC. IT'LL BE SAFE AND WARM...

...AND WE'LL ALL BE TOGETHER.

DON'T WORRY. ANDY'S GONNA TAKE CARE OF US. I GUARANTEE IT.

BUT LATER THAT DAY...

ANDY, IT'S GARBAGE DAY. ANYTHING YOU'RE NOT TAKING TO COLLEGE EITHER GOES TO THE **ATTIC** OR IT'S **TRASH**.

MOM, I'M NOT LEAVING 'TIL FRIDAY.

COLLEGE

YOU NEED TO START MAKING DECISIONS LIKE...THESE TOYS. SHOULD WE DONATE 'EM TO **SUNNYSIDE**?

THE CHILDREN'S DAY CARE? **NO!**

FINE. YOU HAVE 'TIL FRIDAY. ANYTHING THAT'S NOT PACKED FOR COLLEGE OR IN THE ATTIC...

...IS GETTING **THROWN OUT**.

...

WHAT'S HAPPENING, BUZZ?

WE'RE GETTING THROWN OUT, YOU IDIOT! THAT'S WHAT'S HAPPENING!

ANDY?!

OH, NO!

THAT'S NOT TRASH! THAT'S NOT TRASH!!!

RUMBLING UP THE STREET, THE GARBAGE TRUCK IS ALREADY COMING. THERE'S NO TIME TO LOSE!

GASP!

WOODY GRABS A PAIR OF SCISSORS, RUNS TO THE EDGE OF THE WINDOW SILL, LUNGES FOR THE DRAINPIPE, AND SLIDES DOWN.

HE HAS TO OPEN THE BAG TO FREE HIS FRIENDS!

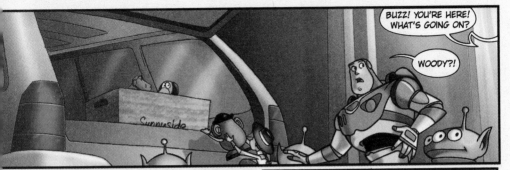

BUZZ! YOU'RE HERE! WHAT'S GOING ON?

WOODY?!

IT'S UNDER CONTROL, WOODY. WE'RE GOING TO **DAY CARE**.

DAY CARE? HAVE YOU ALL LOST YOUR MARBLES?

WELL, *"COLLEGE BOY,"* DIDN'T YOU SEE? ANDY THREW US AWAY!

THAT WAS A MISTAKE, HE WAS PUTTING YOU IN THE ATTIC. ANDY'S MOM THOUGHT YOU WERE TRASH!

YEAH! AFTER HE PUT US IN A TRASH BAG!

ANDY'S MOVIN' ON, WOODY...IT'S TIME WE DID THE SAME.

...

WE CAN HAVE A NEW LIFE HERE, WOODY. A CHANCE TO MAKE KIDS HAPPY AGAIN!

WHY DON'T YOU STAY?

YOU'LL BE PLAYED WITH!

I CAN'T!

LOOK, EVERYONE, IT'S NICE HERE, I ADMIT. BUT WE NEED TO GO HOME!

I **HAVE** A KID! YOU HAVE A KID...**ANDY**! AND IF HE WANTS US AT COLLEGE OR IN THE ATTIC, THAT'S WHERE WE SHOULD BE!

NOW I'M GOING HOME. C'MON BUZZ.

BUZZ?

OUR MISSION WITH ANDY'S COMPLETE, WOODY.

FINE! PERFECT! SO THIS IS IT? AFTER ALL WE'VE BEEN THROUGH?

...

SO WOODY LEAVES, ALONE.

YIKES! PRETTY HIGH!

FWOoO

OH, NO!

A KITE?!

605

...

NO, NO...LOOK, I JUST NEED TO KNOW HOW TO GET OUTTA HERE!

I FOUND THE SPACESHIP!

QUICK! FASTEN YOUR SEATBELTS!

3...2...

...BLAST-OFF!

LOOKING AROUND IN WONDER...

...WOODY FEELS SOMETHING ALMOST FORGOTTEN, SOMETHING HE DIDN'T KNOW HE MISSED SO MUCH.

YOU SAVED US, COWBOY! YOU'RE OUR HERO!

IN THE MEANTIME, AT SUNNYSIDE...

AAAAAH!

MY TAIL! WHERE'S MY TAIL?

SUNNYSIDE DAY CARE. THE CHILDREN HAVE GONE.

WHERE'S MY NOSE?

HERE IT IS...

HERE'S YOUR ARM!

ANDY NEVER PLAYED LIKE THAT!

THESE TODDLERS! THEY DON'T KNOW HOW TO PLAY WITH US!

WE SHOULD BE IN THE BUTTERFLY ROOM WITH THE BIG KIDS!

WE'LL GET THIS STRAIGHTENED OUT...I'LL GO TALK TO LOTSO ABOUT MOVING US TO THE OTHER ROOM!

ALL THE CATERPILLAR ROOM DOORS ARE CLOSED...

...BUT THANKS TO HIS SPACE RANGER AGILITY, BUZZ REACHES THE TRANSOM OVER THE HALL DOOR!

AND FROM THERE HE HEARS SOMETHING SUSPICIOUS...

YOU THINK THEY HAD A FUN PLAYTIME?

SHHH! THEY MIGHT HEAR YOU!

HAHAHA!

HEY, WHAT DO YOU GUYS THINK OF THE NEW RECRUITS? ANY KEEPERS?

NAH, DISPOSABLE!

CHUCK 'EM IN THE LANDFILL!

WE'LL BE LUCKY IF THEY LAST US A WEEK!

ZZ IS SHOCKED. HE'S GOT TO WARN THE OTHERS!

BUT BIG BABY DISCOVERS HIM!

GASP!

WELL, WELL, LOOK WHO WE HAVE HERE!

STOP! LET ME GO!

TAKE HIM TO THE "LIBERRY!"

NOOOOO!

EXCELLENT! I'LL GO GET MY FRIENDS...

WHOA, WHOA! HOLD ON THERE, BOSS! THOSE CATERPILLAR KIDS NEED SOMEONE TO PLAY WITH.

BUT MY FRIENDS DON'T BELONG THERE!

NONE OF US DO! WHICH IS WHY WE ASK THE NEWER TOYS TO TAKE ON THE HARDSHIPS THE REST OF US CAN'T BEAR ANYMORE...

THAT MAKES SENSE, BUT... WE'RE A FAMILY. I'LL STAY WITH THEM.

FAMILY MAN, EH? HOLD HIM!

WHAT ARE YOU...?

AND BRING IN... THE **BOOKWORM!**

AND SO...

HOLD ON...HERE IT IS!

IT WAS FILED UNDER LIGHTYEAR!

LET'S SEE HERE... ACCESSORIES... MAINTENANCE...OH, HERE WE GO!

ACCESSORIES

"REMOVE SCREWS TO ACCESS BATTERY COMPARTMENT..."

WHAT ARE YOU DOING? STOP!

"TO RETURN YOUR BUZZ LIGHTYEAR TO ITS ORIGINAL FACTORY SETTINGS, SLIDE THE SWITCH FROM **PLAY** TO **DEMO**...."

PLAY DEMO

NO! NOOOO!

WHAT WAS THAT?

SOUNDS LIKE IT CAME FROM THE HALL!

I'LL SEE WHAT IT WAS.

POP

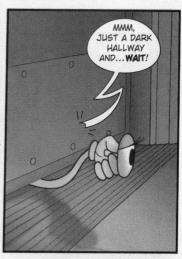

MMM, JUST A DARK HALLWAY AND...**WAIT!**

THIS IS WEIRD...I SEE ANDY! IT'S MY OTHER EYE, THE ONE I LEFT BEHIND, AT HOME!

ANDY'S LOOKING FOR SOMETHING, HE'S SO UPSET... OH, NO! THIS IS TERRIBLE!

INCREDIBLE! THROUGH HER LOST EYE MRS. POTATO HEAD CAN SEE ANDY'S ROOM RIGHT NOW!

HE'S LOOKING FOR US!

WELL, THEN...WOODY WAS TELLING THE TRUTH! ANDY **DOES** WANT US!

GUYS... WE GOTTA GO HOME!

GO?

WHY, YOU JUST GOT HERE! WE WERE RUNNIN' LOW ON VOLUNTEERS FOR THE LITTLE ONES... THEY LOVE NEW TOYS!

!

LOVE?! WE'VE BEEN CHEWED! KICKED! DROOLED ON!

WELL, HERE'S THE THING...YOU AIN'T LEAVIN' SUNNYSIDE.

OH, YEAH? AND WHO'S GONNA STOP US?

BUZZ?!

YOU'RE BACK!

OOOO...

WAAAH

WHAM
POW
BONK

PRISONER DISABLED, COMMANDER LOTSO!

BUZZ? WHAT ARE YOU DOING? WE'RE YOUR FRIENDS!

SILENCE, MINION OF ZURG! YOU'RE IN THE CUSTODY OF THE GALACTIC ALLIANCE!

ZURG?

OH, NO...

GOOD WORK, LIGHTYEAR. NOW LOCK 'EM UP!

LATER, WHEN EVERYONE'S IMPRISONED IN CUBBIES...

LISTEN UP, FOLKS. IF YOU PAY YOUR DUES, LIFE HERE CAN BE A DREAM COME TRUE! BUT IF YOU BREAK OUR RULES, WELL...

...YOU'RE JUST HURTING YOURSELVES.

GASP!

WOODY!

WHAT DID YOU DO TO HIM?!

Y'ALL GET A GOOD NIGHT'S REST! YOU GOT A FULL DAY OF PLAY TOMORROW...

BONNIE'S KITCHEN, A MOMENT LATER...

YES! IT'S RIGHT AROUND THE CORNER!

I'M GOING TO COLLEGE!

IF YOU EVER GET TO SUNNYSIDE DAY CARE, TELL 'EM WOODY MADE IT HOME!

YOU CAME FROM SUNNYSIDE? HOW DID YOU ESCAPE?

WELL, IT WASN'T EASY, I...WHAT DO YOU MEAN, "ESCAPE?"

SUNNYSIDE IS A PLACE OF RUIN AND DESPAIR RULED BY AN EVIL BEAR...A MONSTER!

LOTSO?! BUT...HOW DO YOU KNOW THAT?

"CHUCKLES, TELL HIM."

I AM CHUCKLES AND I KNOW LOTSO. HE WAS A GOOD TOY. A FRIEND...

618

"ME AND HIM, WE HAD THE SAME KID, DAISY."

"DAISY LOVED US ALL, BUT LOTSO...LOTSO WAS SPECIAL."

"ONE DAY, WE TOOK A RIDE, HIT A REST STOP, HAD A LITTLE PLAYTIME."

"AFTER LUNCH, DAISY FELL ASLEEP."

"HER PARENTS TOOK HER HOME AND FORGOT US THERE. THEY NEVER CAME BACK."

"LOTSO WOULDN'T GIVE UP."

"IT TOOK US FOREVER, BUT WE FINALLY MADE IT BACK TO DAISY'S."

"BUT BY THEN..."

"...IT WAS TOO LATE."

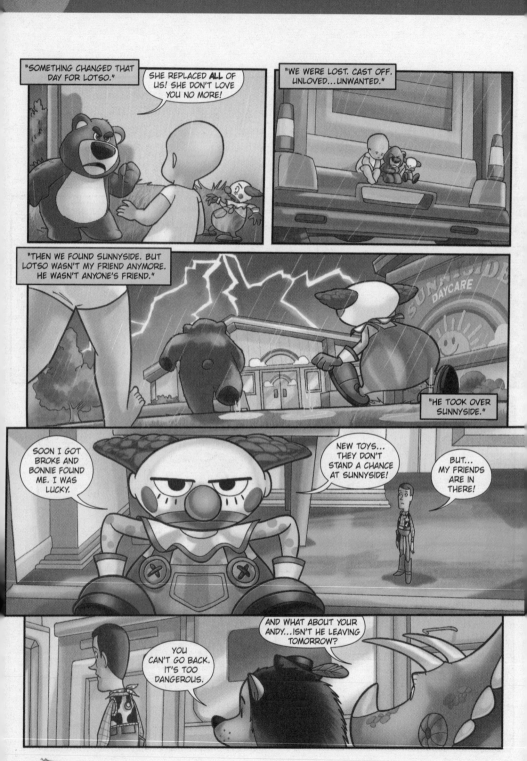

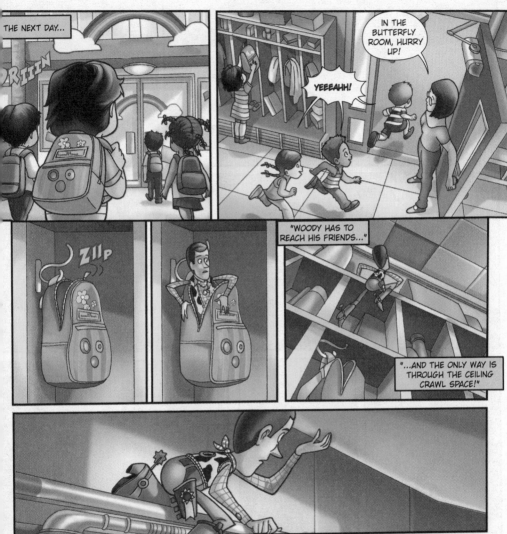

THE NEXT DAY...

IN THE BUTTERFLY ROOM, HURRY UP!

YEEEAHH!

"WOODY HAS TO REACH HIS FRIENDS..."

"...AND THE ONLY WAY IS THROUGH THE CEILING CRAWL SPACE!"

ZIIP

?

KEEP THE BUZZ LIGHTYEAR INSTRUCTION MANUAL AT HAND, BOOKWORM!

A BUZZ MANUAL?

ONE NEVER KNOWS...

OK, CATERPILLAR KIDS! RECESS!

DRIIIN

PSSST! HEY, GUYS!

?

WOODY?!

YOU'RE ALIVE!

OF COURSE I'M ALIVE!

HEY, MY HAT!

AIN'T ONE KID EVER LOVED A TOY, REALLY!

WHAT ABOUT **DAISY**? YOU USED TO DO EVERYTHING WITH HER!

YEAH, THEN SHE ABANDONED US!

SHE LOST YOU! IT WAS **YOU**, LOTSO! **YOU** TURNED YOUR BACK ON HER! YOU LIED TO BIG BABY!

SHA

AND WHEN WOODY TOSSES DOWN THE PENDANT THAT CHUCKLES GAVE HIM...

WHERE'D YOU GET THAT?!

MAMA!

THUNK

SHE NEVER LOVED YOU! DON'T BE SUCH A **BABY!**

CREEEK

PUSH 'EM IN THE TRASH, **STRETCH!** ALL OF 'EM!

BUT BIG BABY KNOWS WOODY IS RIGHT--IT WASN'T DAISY'S FAULT...

WHAT? PUT ME DOWN, YOU **IDIOT**!

...IT WAS LOTSO'S!

AHHHH!

KLANG

HE'S GONE!

C'MON! HURRY! THE GARBAGE TRUCK IS COMIN'!

VROOM

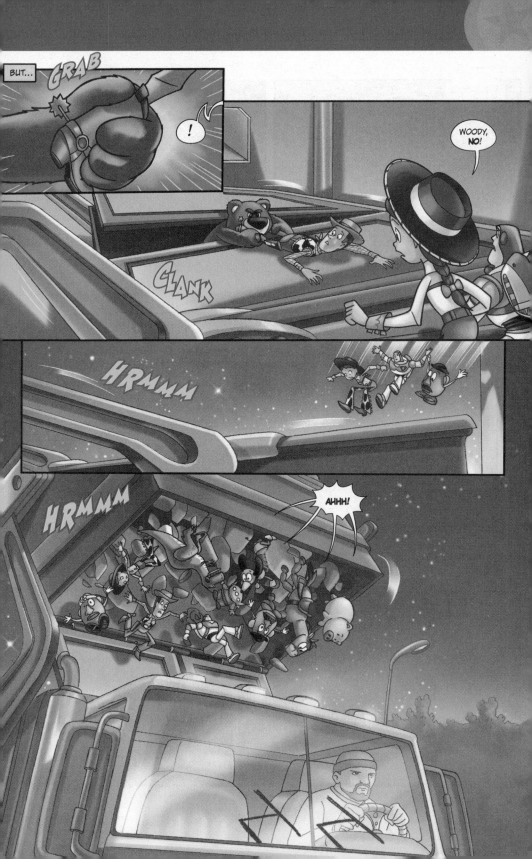

BUZZ, YOU OK? BUZZ!

OOOH...

THAT WASN'T ME, WAS IT?

OU'RE BACK! OU'RE BACK!

WHAT HAPPENED? WOODY, WHY AREN'T YOU WITH ANDY?

I HAD TO RESCUE MY FRIENDS.

WE'RE IN A GARBAGE TRUCK NOW, BUZZ...

"...ON THE WAY TO THE DUMP!"

TRI-COUNTY DUMP

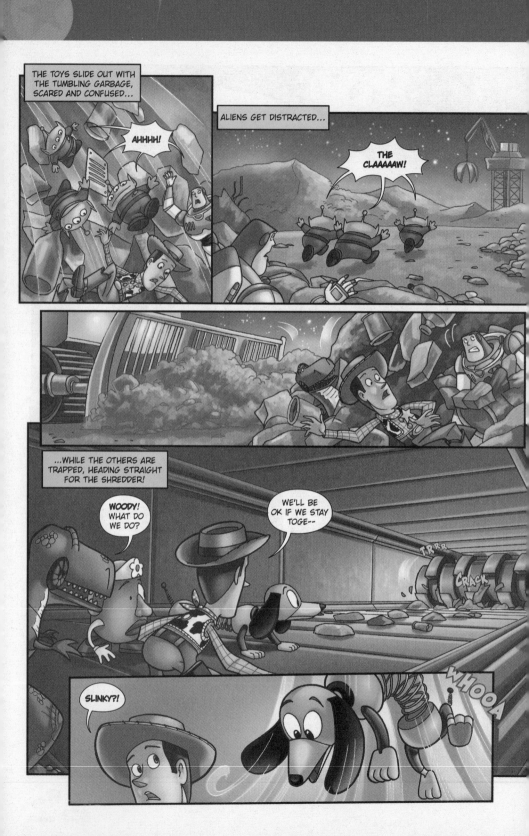

635

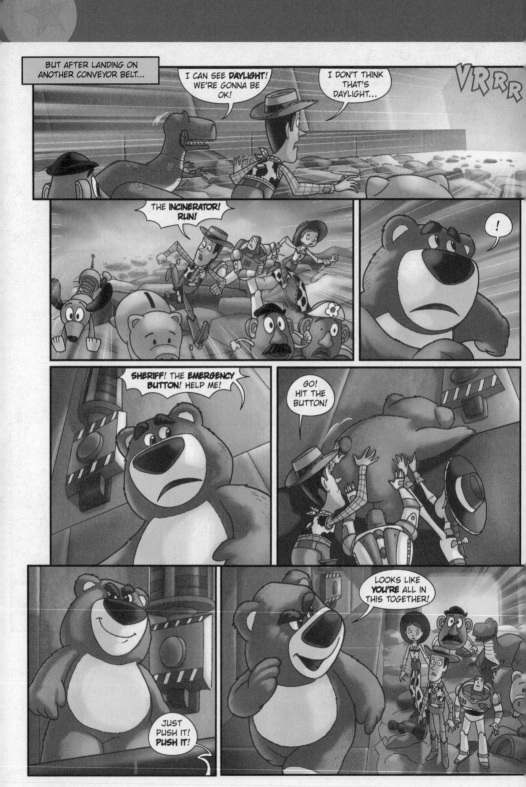

"...E'S NOT WORTH IT."

LOOK WHAT I **FOUND!** I HAD ME ONE OF THESE, WHEN I WAS A **KID**...

THERE YOU GO...

!!!

HEY, BUDDY... Y'MIGHT WANNA KEEP YER **MOUTH SHUT!**

COME ON, WOODY...WE GOTTA GET YOU HOME!

BUT... WHAT ABOUT ...U, GUYS? I MEAN, ...AYBE THE ATTIC'S ...OT SUCH A GREAT IDEA.

WE'RE ANDY'S TOYS...

WE'LL BE THERE FOR HIM. **TOGETHER.**

IT'S MORNING WHEN WOODY AND THE TOYS GET BACK TO ANDY'S HOUSE.

JUST IN TIME TO SAY GOODBYE...

HAVE FUN AT COLLEGE, WOODY!

TAKE CARE OF ANDY!

OH, THERE YOU ARE!

YEAH, SURE...

BACK IN THE COLLEGE BOX, WOODY FEELS UNSETTLED AND ALONE...

...AND IN ONE SELFLESS MOVE HE QUICKLY HOPS OUT OF THE BOX, TO WRITE SOMETHING FOR ANDY.

A NOTE...

DID YOU SAY GOODBYE TO MOLLY?

MOM, WE'VE SAID GOODBYE LIKE TEN TI--

...A SIMPLE, UNEXPECTED NOTE WITH AN ADDRESS...

HEY, MOM-- DO YOU REALLY THINK I SHOULD **DONATE** THIS?

DONATE TO

BONNIE

1225 SYCAMO

641

THE END

SOMEWHERE IN THE NORTH PACIFIC...

...ON A MYSTERIOUS OIL DERRICK...

COME ON, GUYS. THESE CRATES AREN'T GONNA UNLOAD THEMSELVES.

...A SECRET AGENT IS ON A MISSION!

TOO MANY CARS HERE. OUT OF MY WAY!

PROFESSOR Z?

HERE IT IS, PROFESSOR. YOU WANTED TO SEE THIS BEFORE WE LOADED IT?

VRRR

AH, YES. SHOW ME, PLEASE. VERY CAREFULLY.

A TV CAMERA? WHAT DOES IT DO ANYWAY?

NONE OF YOUR BUSINESS!

...UNTIL THEY FINALLY SURROUND HIM ON THE TOP OF THE HELIPAD!

YOU ARE TRAPPED!

IF YOU SAY SO...

FSSSH

SREEEE

RATTA

FALLING INTO THE WATER...

RATTTA

...McMISSILE ELUDES HIS ENEMIES...

HE'LL DROWN!

FINN McMISSILE IS DEAD!

WUNDERBAR. WITH FINN McMISSILE GONE, WHO CAN STOP US?

...AND ESCAPES!

ZMMM

THAT NIGHT, AFTER A WHOLE DAY OF FUN...

...LIGHTNING McQUEEN AND SALLY ARE ENJOYING A ROMANTIC EVENING TOGETHER AT THE WHEEL WELL RESTAURANT.

MATER IS TAKING CARE OF THE DRINKS...

...WHILE EVERYBODY ELSE'S ATTENTION IS DIRECTED TOWARD "THE MEL DORADO SHOW!"

HE SOLD HIS OIL FORTUNE, CONVERTED HIMSELF INTO AN ELECTRIC CAR, AND DEVOTED HIS LIFE TO FINDING A RENEWABLE, CLEAN-BURNING FUEL!

...HE'S CREATED A RACING COMPETITION LIKE NO OTHER--THE FIRST WORLD GRAND PRIX!

WELCOME, SIR MILES AXLEROD!

allinol
ALL FOR ONE

NOW HE CLAIMS TO HAVE DONE IT!

...AND TO SHOW THE WORLD WHAT HIS NEW SUPERFUEL CAN DO...

THANK YOU, MEL.

651

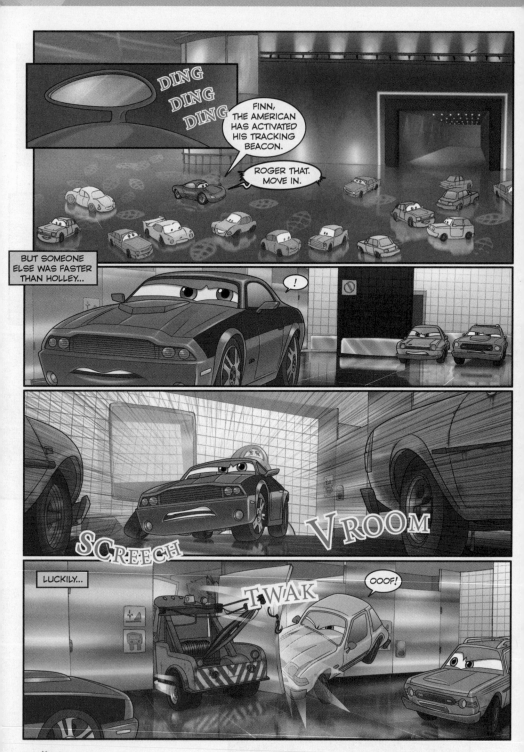

AT LIGHTNING'S PIT, THE CREW IS AT WORK!

HIS SUSPENSION STATS LOOK GOOD.

TIRE PRESSURE IS EXCELLENT.

HE'S GOT PLENTY OF FUEL.

AND HE'S AWESOME!

WHY IS HE IN THE PITS? HE'S SO EXPOSED.

IT'S HIS COVER. AND ONE OF THE BEST I'VE SEEN, TOO. LOOK AT THE DETAIL OF THAT RUST. IT MUST HAVE COST HIM A FORTUNE.

BUT WHY HASN'T HE CONTACTED US YET?

THERE'S PROBABLY HEAT ON HIM. BE PATIENT.

MEANWHILE, ON A ROOFTOP...

FZZZZT

IT IS TIME.

ROGER THAT, PROFESSOR Z. GOODBYE NUMBER FIVE.

FZZZT

CRRACK

OH! MIGUEL CAMINO HAS BLOWN AN ENGINE!

UNFORTUNATELY, GREM AND THE TV CAMERA AREN'T THE ONLY DANGER...

...AS HOLLEY SOON FINDS OUT!

THE PACER FROM THE PARTY LAST NIGHT...AND THREE OTHER CARS, THEY ARE ALL CROSSING IN ON...

...OH NO!

GET HIM OUT OF THE PITS. NOW!

SECONDS LATER, ON THE TARMAC...

WHOA! THIS IS FIRST CLASS SERVICE!

HEY! YOUR KARATE PARTNERS ARE BACK HERE!

DRIVE FORWARD. WHATEVER YOU DO, DON'T STOP!

WHOOOOOOOOA!

SKREEEE

GRRR

THACK FWOOSH

FWOOSH

FWOOSH

FWOOSH

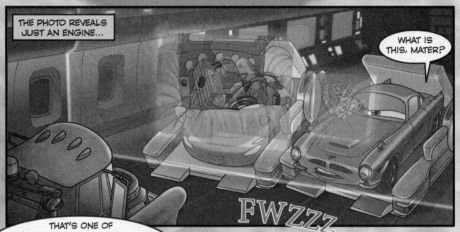

THE PHOTO REVEALS JUST AN ENGINE...

WHAT IS THIS, MATER?

FWZZZ

THAT'S ONE OF THE WORST ENGINES EVER MADE. IT'S AN OLD ALUMINUM V8 ENGINE WITH A LUCAS ELECTRICAL SYSTEM AND WHITWORTH BOLTS.

THIS WAS SUPPOSED TO BE A PHOTO OF THE CAR BEHIND EVERYTHING, NOT JUST AN ENGINE.

I'M NOT HAPPY ABOUT THIS...

WELL THIS GUY MUST BE HAPPY...

...SEE HOW HE HAD MOST OF HIS PARTS REPLACED? THOSE ARE ORIGINAL PARTS. NOT EASY TO COME BY.

RARE PARTS. THAT'S SOMETHING WE CAN TRACK.

WELL DONE, MATER. I KNOW OF A BLACK-MARKET PARTS DEALER IN PARIS...

THE NEXT DAY AT PORTO CORSA, THE SECOND RACE HAS BEGUN...

VROOOM

GET READY, MATER. YOU'RE ON ANY MOMENT NOW.

I DON'T KNOW ABOUT THIS, FINN. I DON'T WANT TO SCREW THINGS UP.

IMPOSSIBLE. JUST APPLY THE SAME DEDICATION YOU'VE BEEN USING TO PLAY THE "IDIOT TOW TRUCK" AND YOU'LL BE FINE!

"IDIOT?" IS THAT HOW YOU SEE ME?

THAT'S HOW EVERYONE SEES YOU! ISN'T THAT THE IDEA? NO ONE REALIZES THEY'RE BEING FOOLED BECAUSE THEY'RE TOO BUSY LAUGHING AT THE FOOL.

ZZZATTT

?!

WHY AREN'T YOU IN DISGUISE? THERE'S NO TIME!

SO, NOW THAT HOLLEY HAS PUT THE REAL IVAN OUT OF COMMISSION...

HOLLEY! WHAT JUST HAPPENED?

CRRACK

I'M DETECTING HIGH LEVELS OF ELECTROMAGNETIC RADIATION...FINN, IT'S THE CAMERA! ON THE TOWER!

FINN RACES TO A ROOFTOP BEHIND THE TOWER...

...AND LEAPS...

WOOOM

...BUT THINGS DO NOT GO AS PLANNED...

THAP THAP THAP FFF THONG

NO!

WE FIGURED YOU MIGHT STOP BY!

MATER! ABORT MISSION! THEY'VE GOT FINN! GET OUT OF...

SCREECH

MATER IS ALONE NOW.

AND NOBODY CAN STOP THE CAMERA...

CRACK CRACK CRACK

IT'S THE END OF THE RACE!

VRROOM

56

LIGHTNING McQUEEN IS THE WINNER! FRANCESCO'S SECOND! BUT THEY HAVE NO IDEA WHAT HAPPENED BEHIND THEM...

LATER, AT THE PRESS CONFERENCE...

I CANNOT CONTINUE TO RISK THE LIVES OF ANY MORE RACE CARS. THE FINAL RACE WILL NOT BE RUN ON ALLINOL!

A TOAST! TO THE DEATH OF ALLINOL AND ALTERNATIVE FUEL FOREVER!

CHEERS

BUT...

MY FUEL FOR THE FINAL RACE WILL BE ALLINOL! MY FRIEND FILLMORE SAYS THE FUEL'S SAFE. THAT'S GOOD FOR ME.

I DIDN'T STAND BY A FRIEND OF MINE RECENTLY...I'M NOT GOIN' TO MAKE THE SAME MISTAKE TWICE.

YES, SIR. OF COURSE.

ALLINOL MUST BE FINISHED FOR GOOD. LIGHTNING MUST BE KILLED!

SHOCKED BY PROFESSOR Z'S WORDS, MATER BACKS UP AND HITS ONE OF THE MONITORS.

NO!

THUNK

UNFORTUNATELY THIS DEACTIVATES HIS DISGUISE PROGRAM...

ZWATTT

IT'S THE AMERICAN SPY! CATCH HIM!

THIS... THIS IS ALL MY FAULT.

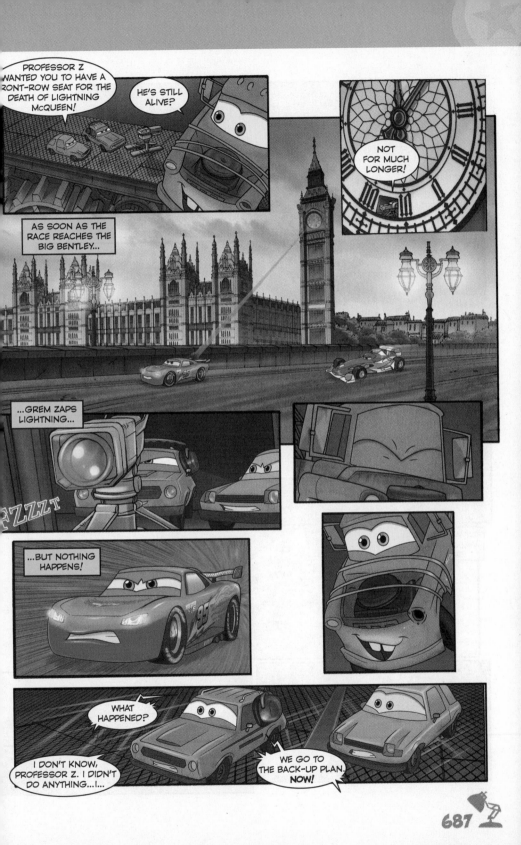

687

BACK-UP PLAN?

WE SNUCK A BOMB IN LIGHTNING'S PIT.

THE NEXT TIME HE MAKES A STOP, INSTEAD OF SAYING "KACHOW" HE'S GONNA GO "KA-BOOM!"

DADGUM LEMONS.

CLACK

REQUEST AKNOWLEDGED: GATTLING GUN!

HE THOUGHT WE WOULDN'T TAKE HIS BULLETS! LET'S GO!

?

TOW

Radial

BUT WHEN ACER AND GREM ARE GONE...

DADGUM!

CLACK

CLACK

CLACK

DADGUM! DADGUM! DADGUM!

SNAP

THEY LAND SAFELY ON THE BIG BENTLEY PLATFORM...

...WHERE THEY MAKE AN AWFUL DISCOVERY!

OH, NO. ISN'T THAT MATER'S AIR FILTER?

I KNEW HIS ESCAPE WAS TOO EASY...HURRY UP, HOLLEY!

CRASH

WOOOM

VROOM

691

CRASH

BONK

THE PROFESSOR'S ON THE RUN! GET LIGHTNING McQUEEN!

HOLLEY! I'LL GET PROFESSOR Z! YOU HELP MATER!

GOT IT, FINN!

WOOM

THEY STRAPPED IT TO ME TO KILL YOU AS A BACK-UP PLAN.

C4 04:08 C4

BACK-UP PLAN? MATER WHO PUT A BOMB ON YOU?

YOU!

WHY DIDN'T MY DEATH RAY KILL YOU?

DEATH RAY?!?

LIGHTYEAR WGP 95 95

TURN OFF THE BOMB, PROFESSOR!

IT'S VOICE ACTIVATED AND CAN ONLY BE DEACTIVATED BY THE ONE WHO ACTIVATED IT.

IT'S NOT ME.

LET GUIDO TRY!

LUIGI?

BUT EVEN WITH AN EXPERT'S TOUCH...

CON QUESTI DADI LE MIE CHIAVI NON FUNZIONANO!

WHAT'S WRONG?

I GET IT! I KNOW WHAT NEEDS TO BE DONE!

NONE OF HIS WRENCHES FIT THE BOLTS!

THEN, MATER, PLEASE DO IT.

BUT NOBODY TAKES ME SERIOUSLY. I KNOW THAT NOW. THIS AIN'T RADIATOR SPRINGS...

IF PEOPLE DON'T TAKE YOU SERIOUSLY THEN THEY NEED TO CHANGE. NOT YOU, MATER. I DIDN'T AND I WAS WRONG.

THANKS, BUDDY.

COMPU-TER...

"...I NEED YOU TO TAKE US SOMEPLACE!"

AHHHH!

WOOSH

SECONDS LATER, ON THE ROYAL BUCKINGHAM PALACE BALCONY...

BACK UP! STAY AWAY!

NO! IT'S OK! MATER HAS SOMETHING IMPORTANT TO SAY!

HOLD YOUR FIRE! YOU COULD HIT THE BOMB!

MATER, TELL THEM WHAT YOU KNOW!

YOUR MAJESTY, SOMEONE'S BEEN SABOTAGING THE RACERS AND HURTING THE CARS AND I KNOW WHO!

IT'S HIM! SIR AXLEROD!

WHAT?? YOU'VE GOT TO BE CRAZY!

I FIGURED IT OUT WHEN I REALIZED YOU ATTACHED THIS BOMB WITH WHITWORTH BOLTS, THE SAME BOLTS...

...THAT HOLD TOGETHER THE OLD BRITISH ENGINE FROM THE PHOTOGRAPH.

AND THEN I REMEMBER WHAT THEY SAY ABOUT OL BRITISH ENGINES: "IF THERE AIN'T NO C UNDER 'EM, THERE AIN'T NO OIL IN 'EM!"

IT WAS YOU LEAKING OIL IN JAPAN, NOT ME!

WHAT ARE YOU TALKING ABOUT? I'M ELECTRIC!

YOU'RE FAKING IT! YOU WANTED ALLINOL TO LOOK BAD SO EVERYONE WOULD GO BACK TO OIL! 'CAUSE YOU OWN THAT HUGE OIL FIELD!

STAY AWAY!

YOU'RE INSANE! DEACTIVATE!

BOMB DEACTIVATED. HAVE A NICE DAY, SIR AXLEROD.

AND THE GUILTY PARTY HAS FINAL BEEN CAPTURED.

BUCKINGHAM PALACE. HERO MATER IS DUBBED A KNIGHT BY THE QUEEN...

AND ALL HIS FRIENDS CAME TO SEE HIM!

THE RADIATOR SPRINGS TEAM CAN FINALLY RETURN HOME...

...WHERE EVERY QUESTION HAS AN ANSWER!

THERE'S ONE THING I STILL DON'T GET... WHY THAT BEAM DIDN'T WORK ON ME? FILLMORE, YOU SAID MY FUEL WAS SAFE...

IF YOU'RE IMPLYING THAT I SWITCHED OUT YOUR ALLINOL FUEL WITH MY ORGANIC BIOFUEL BECAUSE I NEVER TRUSTED AXLEROD, YOU'RE WRONG, MAN.

51237

IT WAS HIM.

ONCE BIG OIL, ALWAYS BIG OIL. MAN.

95

FINALLY, A SPECIAL RACE IS ABOUT TO START...

NO PRESS, NO TROPHY. JUST RACING--TO FIND OUT WHO'S THE WORLD'S FASTEST CAR!

FRANCESCO LIKES IT.

...THE RADIATOR SPRINGS GRAND PRIX!

VROOOOM

FINN, IT'S TIME.

YOU'RE LEAVING ALREADY?

WE'VE GOT ANOTHER MISSION, MATER. WHY WON'T YOU COME WITH US?

SPY OR NO SPY, YOU'RE STILL THE SMARTEST, MOST HONEST CHAP I'VE EVER MET...

WELL, THANKS FINN. BUT... THIS IS WHERE I BELONG.

THE END

"MANY YEARS AGO, WHEN I WAS A WEE GIRL..."

"...ON A PERFECT DAY WITH MY PARENTS..."

"...MY FATHER FERGUS, THE KING, GAVE ME A BOW!"

"BUT AS I STARTED PRACTICING, I SAW SOMETHING IN THE FOREST!"

"SUDDENLY, **MOR'DU** THE BEAR SHOWED UP."

MERIDA...

ONCE, THERE WAS AN ANCIENT KINGDOM RULED BY A WISE KING...

OH, MUM...ANCIENT KINGDOM...

...HE DIVIDED THE KINGDOM AMONG HIS FOUR SONS.

BUT THE OLDEST WANTED TO RULE THE LAND FOR HIMSELF...

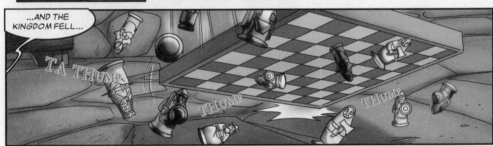

...AND THE KINGDOM FELL...

TA THUMP

THUMP

THUMP

THAT'S A NICE STORY.

IT'S NOT JUST A STORY. LEGENDS ARE LESSONS; THEY RING WITH TRUTH.

MAKE YOUR PEACE WITH THIS. THE CLANS ARE COMING TO PRESENT THEIR SUITORS...

IT'S NOT FAIR!

IT'S MARRIAGE, MERIDA. IT'S NOT THE END OF THE WORLD!

"AND SOON THE DAY ARRIVED..."

SO HERE WE ARE, EHM...THE FOUR CLANS...UH... GATHERING!

"MACINTOSH!"

I PRESENT MY HEIR AND SCION, WHO WITH HIS OWN SWORD VANQUISHED A THOUSAND FOES!

SWISH

"MACGUFFIN!"

I PRESENT MY ELDEST SON, WHO WITH HIS BARE HANDS VANQUISHED **TWO**-THOUSAND FOES!

CRACK

"DINGWALL!"

I PRESENT MY ONLY SON, WHO TOOK OUT A WHOLE ARMADA SINGLE-HANDEDLY!

LIES!!

WHAT? I HEARD THAT! SAY IT TO MY FACE!

709

SO LET THE GAMES BEGIN!

"THERE'S A REASON WHY I CHOSE **ARCHERY**"

"EVEN IF THEY CAN HIT THE TARGET..."

"...EVEN IF THEY CAN HIT A BULLSEYE..."

"...I CAN DO BETTER!"

I AM MERIDA, FIRST-BORN DESCENDANT OF CLAN DUNBROCH! AND I'LL BE SHOOTING FOR MY OWN HAND!

MERIDA! DON'T YOU **DARE**!

FFSSHHH

"I SHOULD HAVE KNOWN...

"...IT WOULDN'T WORK."

YOU DON'T KNOW WHAT YOU'VE DONE! YOU EMBARRASSED THEM! YOU EMBARRASSED **ME**!

IT WILL BE FIRE AND SWORDS IF NOT SET RIGHT.

THIS IS UNFAIR! THIS WHOLE MARRIAGE IS WHAT YOU WANT. DO YOU EVER BOTHER TO ASK ME WHAT I WANT?

YOU ALWAYS TELL ME WHAT TO DO, TRYING TO MAKE ME LIKE YOU. WELL, I'M NOT GOING TO BE LIKE YOU!

YOU'RE ACTING LIKE A CHILD.

AND YOU'RE A...**BEAST**. THAT'S WHAT **YOU** ARE!

NO! STOP THAT!

I'LL NEVER BE LIKE YOU!

RIIIP

MERIDA...

YOU ARE A PRINCESS AND I EXPECT YOU TO **ACT LIKE ONE!**

MERIDA! MERIDA!

OH DEAR...

YOUR BROOM... IT'S SWEEPING BY ITSELF!

THAT'S SILLY. I'M A WIT--I MEAN, A WHITTLER.

SPELLS ARE HER SPECIALTY.

THE CROW TALKS! YOU'RE A WITCH!

YOU'LL GIVE ME A SPELL... IT'S MY MOTHER--

NO, I'M A WOOD CARVER.

GET OUT! SHOO!

WAIT! I'LL BUY IT ALL, EVERY CARVING!

HOW WILL YOU PAY FOR IT?

WITH THIS. I'LL BUY EVERY CARVING...AND ONE SPELL.

I WANT A SPELL TO CHANGE MY MUM, THAT WILL CHANGE MY FATE.

I GOT THIS RING FROM A PRINCE. HE WANTED A SPELL, STRENGTH OF TEN MEN. CHANGED HIS FATE.

"SO, AFTER THE WITCH ACCEPTED THE PAYMENT..."

NOW I NEED JUST A LITTLE BIT OF THIS...

AND THIS...

AND THIS...

HMM... YES!

BOOM

A CAKE? IF MY MUM EATS THIS, SHE WILL CHANGE?

OH, AND WHAT WAS THAT THING ABOUT THE SPELL...STRENGTH OF TEN MEN? OH, WELL...

WAIT! WHAT?! SHE DISAPPEARED...

"I HEADED BACK TO THE CASTLE. I HAD TO GIVE IT A TRY..."

WHERE HAVE YOU BEEN? I WAS SO WORRIED.

I MADE THIS FOR YOU. IT'S A PEACE OFFERING...

YOU MADE THIS FOR ME?

MMM... INTERESTING FLAVOR.

HOW DO YOU FEEL? HAVE YOU CHANGED YOUR MIND ABOUT THE MARRIAGE?

WHY DON'T WE GO UPSTAIRS TO THE LORDS AND PUT THIS WHOLE KERFUFFLE TO REST?

"NOTHING HAPPENED..."

OHH...SUDDENLY, I'M NOT SO WELL.

H-HOW DO YOU FEEL ABOUT THE MARRIAGE NOW?

JUST TAKE ME TO MY ROOM WHILE YOUR FATHER IS ENTERTAINING THE LORDS...

?

A LITTLE TO THE LEFT! THAT'S GOOD! LOOK OUT, YOU MANKY BEAR!

MOR'DU! MOR'DU! MOR'DU!

"...A STORMY NIGHT LONG AGO"

"A HUGE CRACK OF THUNDER FRIGHTENED ME. I RAN TO MUM."

KRACK

A BRAVE WEE LASSIE, I AM HERE.

"I'LL NEVER FORGET HER WORDS."

I'LL ALWAYS BE RIGHT HERE.

"THE MORNING AFTER IS...STRANGE..."

SPUT SPUT

THOSE BERRIES ARE POISONOUS, MUM!

"...IT'S MY TURN TO GIVE THE LESSONS."

HOW DO YOU KNOW YOU DON'T LIKE IT UNLESS YOU TRY IT?

"AND FUNNY..."

"WE FINALLY FIND SOMETHING TO BOND OVER."

"WE ARE HAVING A GREAT TIME.!"

"BUT THEN SOMETHING HAPPENS."

HEY, WHERE ARE YOU GOING?

GRRR

AHH! MUM...?

SNIFF SNIFF

LIKE THE TAPESTRY! THE SPELL HAS HAPPENED BEFORE!

THE OLDEST, THE WILLFUL PRINCE... SPLIT LIKE...

STRENGTH OF TEN MEN... THE INSIDE WILL BECOME THE OUTSIDE...

OH NO! THE PRINCE BECAME...

GRRRR

...MOR'DU!

ROARRR

"WE JUST NEED A WAY INTO THE CASTLE..."

ALL CLEAR...

WHAT'S GOING ON?

NO MORE TALK! NO MORE TRADITIONS! WE SETTLE THIS NOW!

NONE OF YOUR SONS ARE FIT TO MARRY MY DAUGHTER!

YAAAAH

THEN OUR ALLIANCE IS OVER! THIS MEANS WAR!

THEY'RE GOING TO MURDER EACH OTHER!

OUR CLANS WERE ONCE ENEMIES, BUT WHEN WE WERE THREATENED FROM THE SEA, YOU JOINED **TOGETHER** TO DEFEND OUR LANDS.

IT WAS AN ALLIANCE FORGED IN BRAVERY AND FRIENDSHIP.

BUT I'VE BEEN SELFISH. I TORE A GREAT RIFT IN OUR BOND. AND I KNOW I HAVE TO MEND MY MISTAKE.

SO I ACCEPT THE TRADITION AND PLEDGE TO MARRY INTO ONE OF YOUR CLA...

"I'M ABOUT TO SAY IT..."

"...WHEN MUM STARTS MIMING SOMETHING TO ME!"

OR PERHAPS THERE'S ANOTHER WAY? THAT WE MIGHT DARE TO... BREAK TRADITION?

THE QUEEN FEELS WE SHOULD BE FREE TO...WRITE OUR OWN STORY.

UH...

?

MUM? MUM, YOU'VE GOT TO RUN...

BEAR!

IT'S MUM! IT'S YOUR WIFE ELINOR!

YOU'RE TALKING NONSENSE!

IT'S THE TRUTH! THERE WAS A WITCH...AND A SPELL...IT'S NOT MOR'DU!

MOR'DU OR NOT, I'LL AVENGE YOUR MOTHER. AND I'LL NOT RISK LOSING YOU, TOO!

NO, DAD! YOU CAN'T! IT'S YOUR WIFE!

MAUDIE! KEEP THIS AND DON'T LET HER OUT!

HYAH!

"I HAVE TO HELP MUM."

MAUDIE, I NEED YOU!

UH? OH NO...

"I REALLY MESSED UP THIS TIME, BUT MAYBE..."

"...THEY CAN HELP ME AGAIN!"

AHHH.!

GET THE KEY!

HUF HUF

GASP!

"MEANWHILE..."

NOW I NEED NEEDLE AND THREAD...

"...AND THE TAPESTRY!"

I DON'T UNDERSTAND. I RESTORED WHAT WAS TORN. WHY HAVEN'T YOU CHANGED?

...

I MENDED THE BOND... DIDN'T I?

OH MUM, I'M SORRY... THIS IS ALL MY FAULT! I DID THIS TO YOU... TO US...

YOU'VE ALWAYS BEEN THERE FOR ME. YOU'VE NEVER GIVEN UP! I JUST WANT YOU BACK, MUM!

I LOVE YOU.

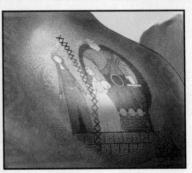

MUM! MUM YOU'RE BACK! YOU'VE CHANGED!

NO, SWEETHEART... WE DID.

ELINOR?!

BOYS?!!

HAHAH

"THE WITCH WAS RIGHT, THERE ARE NO WEE WISHES."

MANY YEARS AGO, WHEN HE WAS JUST AN ELEMENTARY STUDENT...

...MIKE WAZOWSKI VISITED MONSTERS, INC. ON A FIELD TRIP.

I LEARNED EVERYTHING I KNOW FROM MY SCHOOL, MONSTERS UNIVERSITY. IT'S THE BEST SCARING SCHOOL THERE IS!

!

AS THE SCARE ACTIVITY STARTED ON THE SCARE FLOOR, THE KIDS WATCHED IN AWE...

WHOA! LOOK!

HEY! HOW ABOUT WE DO THE TALLEST IN THE BACK?

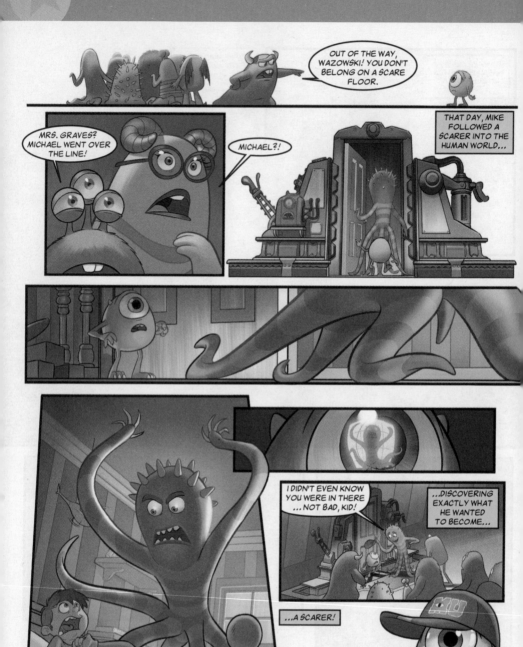

YEARS LATER, MIKE IS OFFICIALLY A STUDENT OF MONSTERS UNIVERSITY...

...DETERMINED TO ENTER THE SCARING SCHOOL AND FULFILL HIS DREAM.

MONSTERS UNIVERSITY ALSO HAS LOTS OF SUPER-COOL CLUBS AND EXTRACURRICULARS...

THEY'RE CRAZY DANGEROUS, SO ANYTHING COULD HAPPEN. YOU CAN TOTALLY DIE.

...AND IT'S WORTH IT! YOU GET A CHANCE TO PROVE YOU'RE THE BEST!

COOL.

SCARE GAMES

FINAL SIGN UP JAN. 25

SCARE GAMES CHAMPIONS

PROVE YOU'RE THE BEST

GOOD MORNING, STUDENTS...

DEAN HARDSCRABBLE, THIS IS A PLEASANT SURPRISE!

WELCOME TO SCARING 101. I'M PROFESSOR KNIGHT!

SHE'S A LEGEND! SHE BROKE THE ALL-TIME SCARE RECORD...

...WITH THE SCREAM IN THAT VERY CAN!

AT THE END OF THE SEMESTER THERE WILL BE A FINAL EXAM...

...FAIL THAT EXAM, AND YOU ARE OUT OF THE SCARING PROGRAM.

759

THAT NIGHT...

WHAT THE--?

ARCHIE? COME HERE BOY...

HEY! WHY ARE YOU IN MY ROOM?

SHHH!

WHERE'D HE GO?!

OVER THERE!

ARCHIE IS FEAR TECH'S MASCOT... I STOLE IT. GONNA TAKE IT TO THE RORS.

THE WHAT?

ROAR OMEGA ROAR? THE TOP FRATERNITY ON CAMPUS? THEY ONLY ACCEPT THE "HIGHLY ELITE"

WHAT AM I DOING? JAMES P. SULLIVAN IS THE NAME.

MIKE WAZOWSKI.

OK, ON THREE, I'LL LIFT THE BED, YOU GRAB THE PIG. READY?

ONE, TWO, THREE!

AHHH!

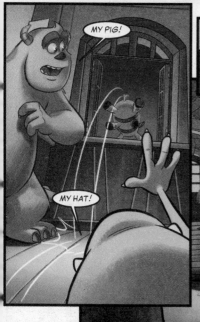

MY PIG!

MY HAT!

CATCH IT, SOMEBODY...

AH!

YEAH! RIDE IT TO FRAT ROW!

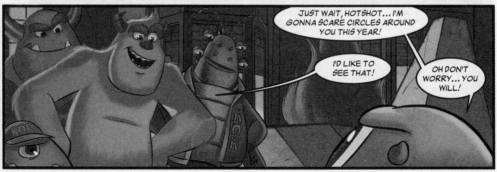

THE DAY OF THE SCARE FINAL...

I'M GONNA WIPE THE FLOOR WITH THAT LITTLE KNOW-IT-ALL TODAY.

YES, YOU ARE, BIG BLUE.

HEY, WAIT, WHAT ARE YOU DOING?

IT'S JUST A PRECAUTION. RORS CAN'T HAVE A MEMBER GETTING SHOWN UP BY A BEACH BALL...

TODAY'S FINAL WILL TEST YOUR ABILITY TO ASSESS A CHILD'S FEAR AND PERFORM THE APPROPRIATE SCARE...

DEAN HARDSCRABBLE IS HERE TO SEE WHO WILL BE MOVING ON IN THE SCARING PROGRAM AND WHO WILL NOT.

WELL... THAT'S SHADOW APPROACH WITH A CRAKLE HOLLER.

DEMONSTRATE.

STOP. THANK YOU.

BUT I DIDN'T GET TO...

I'VE SEEN ENOUGH.

I'M A SEVEN-YEAR-OLD BOY--

ROAR!

I WASN'T FINISHED.

I DON'T NEED TO KNOW ANY OF THAT STUFF TO SCARE.

THAT "STUFF" WOULD HAVE INFORMED YOU THAT THIS CHILD IS AFRAID OF SNAKES. SO A ROAR WOULDN'T MAKE HIM SCREAM...

...IT WOULD MAKE HIM CRY, ALERTING HIS PARENTS, EXPOSING THE MONSTER WORLD, DESTROYING LIFE AS WE KNOW IT.

A NEW SEMESTER STARTS...

SOME SAY THAT A CAREER AS A SCREAM CAN DESIGNER IS BORING...

CRUNCH

CAN TECH

THUMP

SCARE GAMES

PROVE YOU'RE THE BEST

!

SUDDENLY, A PLAN COMES TOGETHER IN MIKE'S MIND...

OUT OF MY WAY!

?

SCARE GAMES

JUST AS THE SCARE GAMES KICK OFF...

AS A STUDENT, I CREATED THESE GAMES AS A FRIENDLY COMPETITION.

BUT BE PREPARED... TO TAKE HOME THE TROPHY YOU MUST BE THE MOST FEARSOME MONSTERS ON CAMPUS.

I'M SIGNING UP!

?

WITH MY BROTHERS OF OOZMA KAPPA...

...THE NEXT WINNING FRATERNITY OF THE SCARE GAMES!

MR. WAZOWSKI, WHAT ARE YOU DOING?

YOU JUST SAID THE WINNERS ARE THE MOST FEARSOME MONSTERS ON CAMPUS. IF I WIN, IT MEANS YOU WERE WRONG!

IF I WIN, YOU LET ME BACK IN THE SCARING PROGRAM.

VERY WELL... IF YOU WIN, I'LL LET YOUR ENTIRE TEAM INTO THE SCARING PROGRAM.

!

BUT IF YOU LOSE, YOU WILL LEAVE MONSTERS UNIVERSITY.

DEAL.

NOW ALL YOU NEED TO DO IS TO FIND ENOUGH MEMBERS TO COMPETE. YOU **NEED** SIX MEMBERS, YOU ONLY HAVE FIVE.

ANYONE ELSE WANT TO JOIN OUR TEAM?

OH SORRY, MIKE. I'M ALREADY ON A TEAM.

YOUR TEAM DOESN'T QUALIFY.

YES IT DOES!

THE STAR PLAYER HAS JUST ARRIVED!

YOU? NO WAY!

BUT MIKE KNOWS HE DOESN'T HAVE A CHOICE...

GAAH! FINE! YES, HE'S ON MY TEAM!

A LITTLE WHILE LATER...

?!

AS THE PRESIDENT OF OOZMA KAPPA, IT IS MY HONOR TO WELCOME YOU TO YOUR NEW HOME!

DON CARLTON, "MATURE" STUDENT.

DON CARLTON
SALES

HI, I'M TERRI WITH AN "I!"

I'M A DANCE MAJOR!

AND I'M TERRY WITH A "Y!"

AND I'M NOT.

I'M ART, NEW AGE PHILOSOPHY MAJOR, EXCITED TO LIVE WITH YOU AND LAUGH WITH YOU AND CRY WITH YOU...

GUESS THAT LEAVES ME.

AH!

MY NAME'S SCOTT SQUIBBLES. MY FRIENDS CALL ME SQUISHY. I'M UNWELCOME PRETTY MUCH EVERYWHERE BUT HERE...

WELL, AS CAPTAIN OF OUR TEAM--

SO YOU GUYS HAVE NO SCARING EXPERIENCE?

NOT A LOT! BUT NOW WE'VE GOT YOU!

YOU'RE ABOUT THE SCARIEST FELLER I'VE EVER SEEN!

AW, THANKS.

WE THOUGHT OUR DREAMS WERE OVER, BUT MIKE SAID IF WE WIN, WE GET INTO THE SCARING PROGRAM!

WE'RE GONNA BE REAL SCARERS!

A LITTLE WHILE LATER...

ARE YOU KIDDING ME?

LOOK, THEY DON'T HAVE TO BE GOOD. I'M GONNA CARRY THE WHOLE TEAM.

REALLY? AND WHO'S GONNA CARRY YOU?

HEY, YOU WANNA GO BACK TO CAN DESIGN, YOU KNOW WHERE THE DOOR IS!

CLIK

GREAT.

THAT NIGHT, OK INITIATES MIKE AND SULLEY IN THE BASEMENT...

DO YOU PLEDGE YOUR SOULS TO THE OOZMA KAPPA BROTHERHOOD?!

WILL YOU TAKE THE SACRED OATH OF THE S--

...WHILE MS. SQUIBBLES DOES THE LAUNDRY!

MOM, WE'RE DOING AN INITIATION!

OH, SCARY! WELL, CARRY ON, JUST PRETEND I'M NOT HERE.

THIS IS MY MOM'S HOUSE...

WELL... YOU'RE IN!

WE KNOW WE'RE NO ONE'S FIRST CHOICE FOR A FRATERNITY, SO IT MEANS A LOT TO HAVE YOU HERE WITH US...

CAN'T WAIT TO START SCARING WITH YOU, BROTHERS!

AND JUST WHEN THEY THINK THEY HAVE SECOND PLACE...

TAKE THAT, WAZOWSKI!

ARE YOU DELIRIOUS? I BEAT YOU!

SECOND PLACE, JAWS THETA CHI!

WHAT?

...THEY FIND OUT THE WHOLE TEAM HAS TO CROSS THE FINISH LINE!

3RD PLACE *EEKS*... 4TH PLACE *PNKS*... 5TH PLACE *HSS*...

NO...NO...

...AND LAST PLACE OOZMA KAPPA!

BUT THEN,...

ATTENTION EVERYONE! JAWS THETA CHI HAS BEEN ELIMINATED FOR ILLEGAL USE OF PROTECTIVE GEL!

OOZMA KAPPA IS BACK IN THE GAMES! IT'S A MIRACLE!

YOUR LUCK WILL RUN OUT EVENTUALLY.

THIS IS GONNA BE HARDER THAN I THOUGHT...

THE SECOND EVENT IS ALL ABOUT STEALTH...

IN THIS EVENT, YOU DO NOT WANT TO GET CAUGHT BY THE LIBRARIAN, YOU MUST MAKE IT OUT WITH THE FLAG.

SULLEY DECIDES THAT HE CAN DO IT BY HIMSELF... AND FAILS.

AHHHHH!

THE LIBRARIAN SPOTS HIM!

BUT...

COME AND GET ME!

HEY, OVER HERE!

HIS TEAMMATES SAVE HIM...

AHHHHH!

... AND DURING THE ESCAPE, SQUISHY USED HIS STEALTH AND GRABBED THE FLAG.

THE OOZMA KAPPA'S ADVANCE TO THE NEXT ROUND!

ALONG WITH THE OTHER TOP SCARE TEAMS, THE *OKS* ARE INVITED TO A PARTY...

OOZMA KAPPA, TONIGHT WE PARTY LIKE SCARERS!

ATTENTION, EVERYONE! THE *ROR* WOULD LIKE TO CONGRATULATE ALL THE TEAMS THAT HAVE MADE IT THIS FAR.

THE *PNKS!* THE *HSS!* AND THE SURPRISE TEAM OF THE SCARE GAMES...

HOORAY!

HOORAY!

...THE OOZMA KAPPA!

SPLASH

FPOP

SNAP

The Campus Roar

'CUTE-MA' KAPPA

IT COULD BE WORSE?

!

HEY, WHAT ARE YOU DOING? STOP MAKING US LOOK LIKE FOOLS!

YOU'RE MAKING YOURSELVES LOOK LIKE FOOLS! LET'S BE HONEST GUYS, YOU'RE NEVER GONNA BE **REAL** SCARERS...

REAL SCARERS LOOK LIKE US! MAYBE YOU CAN WORK IN THE MAILROOM!

CLASSIFIED ADS

HELP WANTED
MAILROOM

MONSTERS, INC.

DON'T LISTEN TO HIM... WE JUST NEED TO KEEP TRYING!

NO, WE NEED TO STOP TRYING! YOU CAN TRAIN MONSTERS LIKE THIS ALL YOU WANT, BUT YOU CAN'T CHANGE WHO THEY ARE!

MIKE, WE APPRECIATE EVERYTHING YOU'VE DONE... BUT HE'S RIGHT, WE'LL NEVER LOOK LIKE THEM.

SORRY, SQUIRT, SOME MONSTERS JUST AREN'T CUT OUT FOR THE BIG LEAGUES.

BIG LEAGUES...

GUYS, WE'RE GOING ON A LITTLE FIELD TRIP!

IF WE GET BACK INTO THE SCARING PROGRAM, I HOPE THERE'S NO HARD FEELINGS.

...AND I KNOW THAT ONE OF YOU IS NOT.

TOMORROW, EACH OF YOU MUST PROVE THAT YOU ARE UNDENIABLY SCARY...

HE WORKS HARDER THAN ANYONE!

DO YOU THINK HE'S SCARY?

HE'S THE HEART AND SOUL OF THE TEAM!

DO YOU THINK HE'S SCARY?

THAT NIGHT SULLEY COACHES MIKE ON HOW TO SCARE...

LET THE ANIMAL OUT!

ROAR!

COME ON, DIG DEEP!

ROAR!

...BUT HE UNDERSTANDS HARDSCRABBLE MIGHT BE RIGHT.

...AND WHILE JOHNNY ALMOST FILLS THE CAN WITH HIS SCREAM...

RRROARR!

AAAAAHHH!

...MIKE PERFORMS A RECORD-BREAKING SCARE!

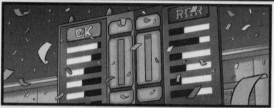

WE'RE IN THE SCARE PROGRAM!

THE OOZMA KAPPA HAVE WON THE SCARE GAMES!

OOZMA! OOZMA! OOZMA!

OOZMA! OOZMA! OOZMA!

LATER...

C'MON BUDDY, WE'RE CELEBRATING!

I DID IT. I CAN'T BELIEVE IT. I'M GONNA BE A SCARER...

YOU HEAR THAT KIDDO? YOU HAVEN'T SEEN THE LAST OF MIKE WAZOWSKI!

BOO!

AAAAHHHH!

?!

I KNEW I WAS SCARY, I DIDN'T KNOW I WAS THAT SCARY...

IT'S BEEN TAMPERED WITH!

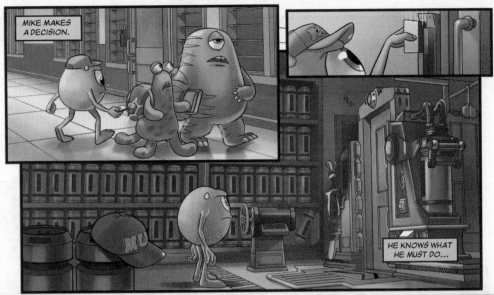

MIKE MAKES A DECISION.

HE KNOWS WHAT HE MUST DO...

...TO PROVE ONCE AND FOR ALL THAT HE'S SCARY!

RRROARR

?

YOU LOOK FUNNY!

?

CAMP TEAMWORK

!

BACK IN THE MONSTERS' WORLD...

MY TEAM HAD NOTHING TO DO WITH IT, IT WAS ALL ME... I CHEATED.

BUT THE ALARM SOUNDS...

EEEEEEE

YOU'RE A DISGRACE TO THIS UNIVERSITY... AND YOUR FAMILY NAME!

SOMEONE BROKE INTO THE DOOR LAB!

NO ONE GOES NEAR THAT DOOR UNTIL THE AUTHORITIES ARRIVE!

IT'S MIKE.

BUT HE COULD DIE OUT THERE! WE GOTTA HELP HIM!

MR. SULLIVAN! DON'T GO IN THERE! IT'S EXTREMELY DANGEROUS!

MIKE?

SULLEY LOOKS FOR HIM INSIDE...

...AND OUTSIDE THE CABIN...

THUMP

...ATTRACTING THE ATTENTION OF THE RANGERS!

A BEAR IN THE CAMP?!

MIKE!

YOU WERE RIGHT, THEY WEREN'T SCARED OF ME.

I THOUGHT I COULD SHOW EVERYBODY THAT MIKE WAZOWSKI IS SOMETHING SPECIAL, AND I'M JUST... NOT.

MIKE AND SULLEY RUN BACK TO THE CABIN...

...BUT THE CLOSET DOESN'T WORK ANYMORE!

UNTIL THE AUTHORITIES ARRIVE, THIS DOOR STAYS OFF.

VVVVVSH

WE'VE GOTTA GET OUT OF HERE!

LET THEM COME! IF WE SCARE THEM, I MEAN REALLY SCARE THEM...

...WE COULD GENERATE ENOUGH SCREAM TO POWER THE DOOR FROM THIS SIDE!

THEY ARE *ADULTS!* I CAN'T DO THIS!

YES YOU CAN, JUST FOLLOW MY LEAD!

AS THE RANGERS ENTER THE CABIN...

AAAAAHHHHH!

RRRROARRR

AAAAAHHHHH!

WORKING TOGETHER, MIKE AND SULLEY COLLECT AN INCREDIBLE AMOUNT OF ENERGY...

...THAT TURNS ON THE DOOR ON THE UNIVERSITY'S SIDE...